◆ HOW TO ROCK

Flash
Training

Eric J. Hörst

CHOCKSTONE PRESS
Evergreen, Colorado

How to Rock Climb: Flash Training

Cover photos:

(front): Ron Kauk on "Tom's Arête" (5.12d), Tuolumne Meadows, California; photo by Beth Wald.

(back): Kurt Smith at "Slice of Life" (5.14a), Rifle, CO; photo by Chris Goplerud. Uncredited photos by author. Instruction photos by author and Mike McGill.

ISBN 0-934641-64-1

Published and distributed by
Chockstone Press, Inc.
Post Office Box 3505
Evergreen, Colorado 80437-3505

Dedication

To my parents, for 30 years of love and support,

and

to Jeff Batzer, my original training partner whose brilliant climbing – in all its forms – continues to be an inspiration.

Jeff Batzer bouldering at Governor Stables, PA, circa 1981.

Acknowledgments

I would like to thank all those who have contributed some of their finite allotment of time and energy to the making of *Flash Training*. In particular, I wish to thank the many expert climbers who enthusiastically shared their knowledge for the benefit of the general climbing population including Mia Axon, Russ Clune, John Gill, Jonathan Houck, Lynn Hill, John Long, Suzanne Paulson, Steve Petro, Mike Pont, Dr. Mark Robinson, Todd Skinner, Kurt Smith, Glenn Thomas, Tim Toula, and Barbara Branda Turner.

I'd also like to thank the photographers and artists whose work graces the pages of this book including John Barstow, John Dine, Stephen Dirnhofer, Chris Falkenstein, Vincent Fasano, Chris Goplerud, Mark Guider, Nina Isabelle, Michael Kodus, Peter Lewis, Mike McGill, Sean Michael, Susan Robinson, Carl Samples, and Rick Thompson. In addition, I must thank Scott Titterington for a great copyedit. Finally, many thanks to other "support team" members. They are Bob Africa, George Mummert, and Bob Perna – thanks for helping to build my outrageous training "box."

And of course, special thanks to my wife Lisa and my parents, Bob and Ethel Hörst.

Life is either a daring adventure or nothing.
Helen Keller

Preface

Flash Training has been in the works for some time – I guess you could say I began my research 17 years ago when my older brother Kyle led me up my first climb, a 5.3. That outing was all it took for me to become enamored of the kinesthetic feel, aesthetics, and spirit of the sport. That day I began my search for the secrets of the higher grades.

Soon after, I met two other high school students from the area, Jeff Batzer and Hugh Herr, who were similarly into climbing. Jeff and I climbed almost daily, and on occasion we met Hugh at the crags for what became our first experience with "competitive" climbing. The major revelation that season was the discovery of *Master of Rock*, the biography of John Gill, which became a sort of "Bible" for our generation of climbers. It was this book that planted the training seed in us. The rest is history.

Master of Rock not only documented the life of the greatest boulderer of all time, it also provided the first tangible information on training for climbing. This was critical because climbers have long been loaded with desire but lacking in hard facts on how to get better. After all, the key to excellence in any field is the coupling of above-average desire and dynamic knowledge.

The goal of this book is to be an accurate resource covering all aspects of climbing performance. This book brings you techniques, ideas, and advice straight from the mouths of over a dozen leading climbers and other professionals. What's more, our ongoing search for new and improved material will yield an updated volume of the book in the future. All of this sets *Flash Training* apart.

I hope that this book will lift you to new heights of motivation and positiveness that will result in new performance heights in your climbing career. Please write and tell us about your breakthroughs on the rock and in the gym, and I encourage you to take the fitness test contained in the Appendix and send it to *Flash Training*. If it weren't for the large, positive response from my training seminars, personal training programs, past articles in *Climbing, Rock & Ice*, and *Flash Communique* training journal, this book might not have come to exist. So by all means drop me a note!

And don't forget to share your energy, abilities, and information with other climbers. Lend them your book for a few days, but make sure you get it back. Remember the old adage, "the teacher learns far more than the students."

A DEFINITION OF TRAINING

Walk around any crag, climbing gym, or group of two or more climbers and you are likely to hear the word "training" flying around like dynos on a route at Rifle. But just what does training mean? For most, training is synonymous with building strength. Undoubtedly, some people expect this book to contain page after page of exercises designed to build muscular strength. Upon first inspection, they may be surprised to notice that only one chapter is focused specifically on "strength training."

I have my own definition of training; it is any practice, discipline, or exercise designed to increase one's efficiency and proficiency on the rock. Clearly, this represents a broad spectrum of subjects and hence the actual content of this book.

Through this paradigm I hope you will accept that training includes many issues, including bouldering to learn problem solving, climbing on a home wall to improve technique, on-sighting, hangdogging, or for that matter, any climbing on real rock, and traveling to experience many different types of climbing. Also included are stretching for flexibility, watching your diet so that you have lots of energy but don't get fat, visualizing a route you are "working," resting sufficiently and listening to your body to avoid injury, evaluating yourself constantly to determine your true physical and mental strengths and weaknesses, and of course, performing various gym exercises that closely relate to the positions and movements common to climbing.

As you can see, strength training is just one piece in the performance puzzle. But how big of a piece? Well, it's hard to say for sure, but I contend that it is certainly not the largest!

This may shock many climbers because their real-life experiences with failure on a climb always seem to center around a lack of strength. But what about all the underlying causes that may have led to premature fatigue? Poor footwork, bad body positioning, over-gripping of holds, climbing too slowly, dismal focus, lack of energy due to poor diet, and dehydration from too much beer and too little water are just a few possible causes.

The moral of the story is that the best training programs for climbing include lots of climbing! Three or four days a week on rock, or an artificial wall is more important and more advantageous than spending those days exercising in the gym. Evidence of this is the fact that climbers who religiously strength train at home tend to lose pure strength while on a long climbing trip, but at the same time realize an increase in climbing performance. Their gains in skill from climbing more frequently outweigh their losses in strength.

This is not to say that you can simply climb a lot and ignore all the other facets of performance. The best climbers clearly focus on putting the complete puzzle together, and this undoubtedly includes frequent strength training.

I have written this book with the hope of furthering your knowledge in the many areas that affect climbing performance. Read the book cover-to-cover, and refer back to it regularly to keep the ideas and techniques fresh in your mind. Apply the information, train hard and smart, and decide to flash!

WARNING: CLIMBING IS A SPORT WHERE YOU MAY BE SERIOUSLY INJURED OR DIE

READ THIS BEFORE YOU USE THIS BOOK.

This is an instruction book to rock climbing, a sport which is inherently dangerous. You should not depend solely on information gleaned from this book for your personal safety. Your climbing safety depends on your own judgment based on competent instruction, experience, and a realistic assessment of your climbing ability.

There is no substitute for personal instruction in rock climbing and climbing instruction is widely available. You should engage an instructor or guide to learn climbing safety techniques. If you misinterpret a concept expressed in this book, you may be killed or seriously injured as a result of the misunderstanding. Therefore, the information provided in this book should be used only to supplement competent personal instruction from a climbing instructor or guide. Even after you are proficient in climbing safely, occasional use of a climbing guide is a safe way to raise your climbing standard and learn advanced techniques.

There are no warranties, either expressed or implied, that this instruction book contains accurate and reliable information. There are no warranties as to fitness for a particular purpose or that this book is merchantable. Your use of this book indicates your assumption of the risk of death or serious injury as a result of climbing's risks and is an acknowledgement of your own sole responsibility for your climbing safety.

C O N T E N T S

Eric Hörst on
"Visionaire" (5.13), Safe
Harbor, Pennsylvania

Mike McGill photo

FLASH TRAINING

ERIC J. HÖRST

Motor Learning and Performance

CHAPTER 1

Take infinite pains to make something that looks effortless.
Michelangelo

Climbing is a demanding sport. It requires physical capabilities such as strength and endurance. It also demands the development of special skills—such as technique, balance, problem solving, hold recognition, and so on. Both fitness and skill must be used in situations of risk with its fear, anxiety and stress.

In recent years, especially with the ascent and dominance of sport climbing, people have been exposed to an increasing amount of information about physical-fitness training for climbing. Methods for improving strength, endurance, cardiovascular capacity, flexibility, and even body composition (weight and fat content) have been widely published. To a lesser extent, there also has been some coverage of the psychological techniques for dealing with fear, failure, self-image, motivation, etc.

Interestingly, the huge and perhaps crucial middle ground—the study of the acquisition of skill, the efficient and rational scheduling of practice and the development of technique and problem solving—has been all but ignored. Consequently, I was happy (psyched!) to receive an excellent primer on the subject of Motor Skills and Learning from Dr. Mark Robinson.

I hope it will serve to initiate some interest in this field. I am certain that climbers would do well to study this neglected topic.

MOTOR SKILLS AND LEARNING

Mark Robinson, M.D.

I became interested in this field, the key to climbing and life in general, during some long and in-depth conversations with Lynn Hill and Russ Clune in the late 1980s. The subject also surfaced when studying the process of the recovery of performance after injury in Sports Medicine. It became apparent to me that the field of Motor Learning was fundamental to any discussion or study of climbing performance.

(page opposite)
Eric Hörst crankin' in the Frankenjüra, Germany.

Mike McGill photo

Sue McDevitt on "Crimson Cringe" (5.12a), Yosemite.

Chris Falkenstein photo

But before I introduce you to the subject of Motor Skills and Learning, let me first point out a few fallacies that have been common to discussions about climbing performance.

Don't Believe the Hype

If I jack up my motivation to fanatic levels and train like mad, I can climb anything.

This is obviously ridiculous, but lots of people act as though it were true. It courts the risk of overuse injury. Of course, it often seems as though the lack of strength and endurance is what limits climbing because muscle failure is the final common pathway by which bad technique, inflexibility or any other fault leads to a fall or failure.

The above idea ignores skill and concentrates only on fitness and desire. Besides, there is a fundamental problem: Everybody is born with certain limitations! There are very many, perhaps thousands, of independent fundamental capacities. Some are physical, such as height and "ape-index," and are not modifiable. Others, such as muscle fiber type and distribution and body proportions, also affect climbing potential and are only able to be improved minimally by training.

Fortunately, a few things are changeable. They include strength, endurance, anaerobic capacity, and body composition. These modifiable factors of performance may be developed and improved but only within limits set by the underlying capacities.

On the basis of study, only about one person per thousand has the innate capacity to develop through training the aerobic qualities needed to enter the ranks of elite endurance athletes. Thus, it would seem that few people have the capacity to acquire the ferocious grip strength needed for 5.14 climbing no matter what their level of motivation and training (grip strength seems to be strongly determined by genetics).

If I perform the training program of an elite climber, then my climbing performance will improve rapidly.

This, too, is wrong and quite dangerous. Each person is born with a different value for each of the many underlying factors (capacities) involved in any given sport. One person may have what it takes for an extremely acute sense of body position. Another may be gifted with a forearm architecture and muscle composition that provide great finger strength or endurance. A third may be gifted with a mind that allows quick perception of possible moves and unexpected, imaginative ways. Some may lack the brains to be afraid of falling. Elite climbers probably have been lucky enough to be born with almost all of these.

Despite this, many rock stars want to attribute their success to large amounts of physical training. This then spurs fledgling climbers to seek out and perform the high-intensity, often dangerous training rituals of the stars, while all along ignoring the most fundamental subject of Motor Skills and Learning (training technique).

Motor Learning – An Overview

Motor Learning, that is to say the process of acquiring some skill of body movement such as walking, writing, talking, or sports skills, occurs in three identifiable and overlapping stages. They may be described as cognitive, motor, and autonomous. The first of these is the "Cognitive Stage."

Cognitive Stage

This stage involves thinking about the activity, listening to explanations of it or comparisons to other familiar things, imaginative projection of what it may be like to do it, visual or kinesthetic anticipation of action, a formulation of the goals or desired results of actual performance.

Early attempts in this stage are clumsy, inefficient, jerky, and expend energy and strength in wasteful ways. It is what you experience when making the first few attempts on a hard (for you) sport route. You look at the route, try to figure out the moves and rest positions, then attempt to climb it, perhaps bolt-to-bolt or on top-rope.

The expected result of early attempts at any skilled activity is imperfect execution, failure in a sense. With continued attempts (practice), the quality of performance improves.

The underlying capacities involved in this stage are largely intellectual and character related and less physical. Thus, people who enjoy early success, who have "natural talent" often seem unlikely and diverge quite a lot from the usual expected body type of the hardman. (This may also explain why climbing used to be populated by eccentrics, mathematical/physics types, etc., in its early days and now is dominated by surfer/skater and health-club/hard-body types.) The old assumption that gymnasts, with their incredible strength and motor skills, would instantly and effortlessly become excellent climbers has not proven true. Although the sports obviously share certain requirements, gymnastics tends to be very stereotyped and repetitive whereas climbing can be quite open and variable and thus based in part on markedly different underlying capacities.

Motor Stage

The next piece of Motor Learning is the "Motor Stage." This stage is less a product of self-conscious effort and thought and more one of automatic increases in the efficiency and organization of the activity by the nervous system, including the brain, as it responds to continued practice. A groove is developed. Multiple attempts and feedback from multiple sources, internal and external, provide a more reliable and effective execution. The energy expended decreases and the natural inertia of the body and limbs are used to advantage.

In the sport climb example, this stage is represented by the attempts at redpoint when the moves and clips are known and the goals are to develop efficiency and to preserve power and endurance for the cruxes. The underlying factors involved in this stage differ from those that lead to early success. They involve the sensitivity of internal movement sensors, the accuracy of limb movement and speed of correction and detection of minor errors, the sensitivity of the performance to anxiety or doubt, etc. These things are obviously less available to conscious awareness or control.

In this stage, the goal of action becomes more refined and demanding. The moves must be done well and efficiently with strength to spare, not eked out, gasping at the verge of nausea or pulped tips. Early, crude success should not be accepted since it will not lead to the best ultimate development of technique and efficiency. Having demanding goals has been shown experimentally to produce both better performance and faster gains. The goal should be to dominate at, say 12a, not just get by at it.

Autonomous Stage

The final stage is called the "Autonomous Stage." At this point, the actions are automatic and require almost no conscious attention. Movement has reached a stable and polished form. You can often do other things while in this state, for instance you can carry on a conversation while driving a car. This is also the elusive "flow state" so often touted by elite athletes – in climbing it is reached only by years of extreme dedication, practice, and discipline.

Another characteristic of this stage is that the mind can move far ahead of the immediate action, like a chess Grandmaster thinking six moves ahead. To the outside observer, individual style and artistry now become noticeable.

In the sport climb example, this stage can be experienced on the successful redpoint, but it more often occurs on the umpteenth repetition of a route that has been ruthlessly wired or during on-sight climbing by a confident and experienced person climbing well below the climber's maximum.

Discerning Skill and Fitness

What I once had to be in top shape to do, I can now do when out of shape (e.g., 5.10 if I'm a 5.12 climber).

What was once the top level for fit, elite climbers (e.g., 5.11) is now commonplace and learned quickly by many people.

Very fit people can be surprisingly bad climbers, and very unfit people can be surprisingly good climbers.

These odd facts help in the understanding of climbing achievement. When making a distinction between fitness and skill, we see that some people are highly skilled and able to climb well even when unfit, while some fit people will always lack in skill. But beyond that, is there any relationship between the two? Does great strength open up a wider range of possible skills or does it foster bad technique?

Definition of Practice and Training

Answering this question requires the two concepts of practice and training. To "practice" is to repeatedly perform the same activity with the idea of improving overall performance of that specific activity. For example, a baseball player hits balls over and over with the goal of honing his skill at batting. Similarly, climbers should practice by climbing a lot with the specific goal of improving climbing skill.

"Training," on the other hand, involves both practice as defined above along with other numerous activities not the same as the primary activity, which are nevertheless done in the belief that they will improve performance of the primary activity. They include such things as weightlifting, running, dieting, etc. These other activities are valid forms of training when they do improve the performance of the primary activities. However, it is surprising how many things done for climbing are not valid training!

Practicing To Improve Skill

Practice follows the "Law of Practice" according to which the quality of performance improves rapidly when the exercise is begun from its baseline level and continues to improve in ever-smaller amounts, approach some ultimate (personal) best performance. This improvement can continue for years, even for very simple tasks such as shown by a famous study of cigar rollers. Skill increases noticeably for years (seven for the cigar rollers). For complex tasks like climbing, the acquisition of skill can likely improve for decades.

This relationship holds fairly well even in surprising circumstances. For one thing, it implies that even after a layoff, skill level will not drop. This has, in fact, been

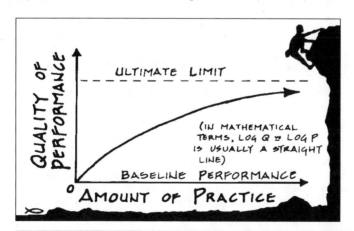

observed. If you rode a bike as a child, you can still ride it. For activities involving little or no fitness, retention of skill is near perfect after a brief warm-up period of a few minutes or hours, depending on the skill. If you once drove a clutch transmission, you will quickly resume your former level of skill in a few hours even after years of driving automatic transmission vehicles. It seems that motor skills are "hard wired" into the brain and never broken or corroded until old age. Thus, many elements of climbing skill, especially such things as slab routes, routes that have been "wired," etc. are not lost with advancing middle age despite upsetting losses of strength, eyesight, abdominal tone, and information-processing ability. There is even some laboratory evidence for this "hard wire" idea.

In one study, rats (the usual victims) were taught how to walk a slack chain. Certain areas of the rat's brain involved in motor control were later shown to have marked increases in nerve-cell connections absent in untrained rats. Thus, practice actually changes the structure of the brain and these structural changes remain in place for later use, even if left unused for years.

If physical fitness is required, the quality of performance will go down during a layoff as strength, etc. are lost through

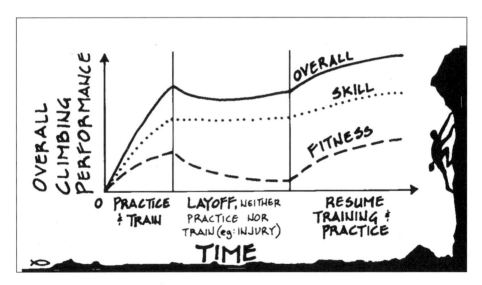

deconditioning and atrophy. That portion of performance due to fitness will return after the layoff or injury only as fitness is regained.

Keep in mind that all of the many elements of fitness – strength, endurance, cardiovascular capacity, flexibility, body fat, etc. – behave differently and respond in various complex and interdependent ways to things such as diet, exercise and rest. Each may diminish quickly; however, as a rule they can be regained, depending on the extent of loss, in a few weeks or months.

Relationship Between Skill and Fitness

For a beginning climber in the Cognitive Stage of Motor Learning, a low level of fitness can pose problems. A certain level of strength is necessary in order to do enough climbing just to begin practice and to develop skill. On the other hand, too much strength allows the beginner to get by with inefficient, wasteful moves which will prevent the development of good technique, unless, of course, the strong person makes good technique a goal instead of just getting up the route.

The problem is further enhanced by the fact that people tend to develop their talents disproportionately. Strong people most likely lift weights. Flexible people probably stretch, and skillful people undoubtedly climb a lot. For most, the drudgery of working on weak points tends to be discouraging.

In fact, much of what may seem to be strength gains in beginners may well represent learning. Even in weightlifting, the amount of weight that can be lifted goes up dramatically in the first week or two. During this period, no measurable change occurs in the muscles used. Familiarity with the exercise, increases in efficiency, and the neurological organization of the movement produce the apparent gains in "strength."

Elite climbers, though, have relatively little to gain from practicing familiar forms of climbing. For those few expert climbers way out on the practice curve near their ultimate skill potential, fitness becomes the crucial factor in performance. Hence, we see the common phenomenon of articles by highly accomplished climbers describing seemingly lethal or disastrously stressful fitness regimes that are sure to plunge the ordinary climber into despair, the doctor's office, or self-defeating over-reliance on fitness as the key to improvement.

For the ordinary climber, it becomes obvious that practicing to improve skill is more important and productive than training for fitness. This is confirmed by the fact that grades that used to be the realm of the fit elite (e.g., 5.11) are now achieved by Elvis-legged bumblies on a wall in the corner of the local health spa! Of course, some of the overall elevation of standards is due to better shoes and chalk, but I think most of it is due to better learning and to having more effective techniques to learn.

Focused fitness training is important after a layoff, a fact that leads many people to believe it is more important than it is. The rapid loss of strength that occurs when heavy workouts are stopped also helps build this belief. Despite this, the most long-term and significant improvements are undoubtedly the result of practice until very late in the average climbing career, when sport-specific strength truly becomes a limitation.

The permanence of skill and rapid variability of fitness is good news to people who must take time off to resolve an injury or for some other reason.

Transference of Skill

In Motor Learning, the idea of transference relates to how practice or skill in one activity accelerates or improves learning of some other perhaps related activity. One startling, but apparently consistent, result in this field of study is that transfer is usually either absent or quite small, even between seemingly similar activities. (When it is seen it is usually in the Cognitive Stage of learning and is small even then). In this way, the complexity, coordination, and integration of skilled movement is so specific that it can derive very little help from other skilled movements. Therefore, only climbing (practice) will improve skill, technique, balance, etc. Horsing around on slack chains, doing one-arm handstands, playing Hacky-sack, and surfing are at best of minimal utility and a waste of time for the purpose of improving climbing skill.

Developing A Wide Range of Schemas

Climbing skill and technique are specific to the kind of rock and terrain on which they are done, but there are good reasons to seek a wide experience, even if your interests are narrowly focused on one type of climbing. This relates to what is called a schema by Motor Learning scientists or what are called engrams by some people.

A schema is a set of rules, usually developed and applied unconsciously by the motor system in the brain and spinal cord, relating how to move and adjust muscle forces, body position, etc., given the parameters at hand. These parameters include, in the case of climbing, the steepness of the rock, its friction qualities, the holds being used, and the kind of terrain (roof, corner, etc.). The more practice and experience you have, the more complete are these rules and the wider the range of situations to which they apply.

People who limit themselves to one climbing area will gain experience at only a narrow range of rock friction, hold types, terrain, etc. The rules they develop will apply only to this kind of situation and will not even do particularly well at the outer ranges of their own chosen specialty. When they travel to new areas, they will end up climbing at a much lower grade or flailing on routes of the grade they were accustomed to at their home area. On the other hand, we have seen how well-traveled climbers could show up at relatively insular areas such as Smith Rocks in the '80s, and the Gunks in the '60s and '70s and do all the hard routes in record time, and then go on to establish new standards. By climbing at a large number of areas and on many different rock types, these climbers developed a large library of schema.

"If one of the international sport climbing competitions were staged on an overhanging 5.13 off-width, we'd probably see contestants trying to paw the bald face on either side of the crack." – John Long, *How To Rock Climb!*

I once had an experience with a top boulderer at a local spot in California. This man could do incredible problems in his local area that very few others could repeat, however, it was obvious that his abilities were limited because he had difficulty climbing 5.10a on his very infrequent road trips. The surprising extent of his limits became apparent one day when he went to show us one of the "easier" problems at his area. He twirled and pranced effortlessly up to a recently broken hold, then flew off. He had grabbed at where the hold used to be in an artful-looking blind move, only to land on his butt. By the next week, most other local boulderers, some of only average ability, had worked out a new sequence. But not our hero. His limited number of schema had limited him once again.

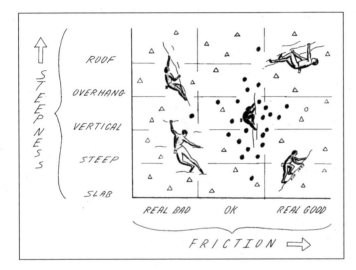

Steepness and friction can be defining parameters for climbers. Those with wide experience will develop good schemas useable in a wide range of possibilities (triangles). These athletes can easily fine tune the schemas to the demands of a particular area. Specialists (circles) will have very narrow schemas – all but useless in unfamiliar territory.

Experiments in Motor Learning seem to show that people who seek out great variety in practice will eventually outperform specialists, even at their own chosen ground. Thus, while off-width practice may perhaps be too far afield to help the usual sport climbing competitor, a wide variety of climbing will.

Variable Practice

One related method to help acquire a comprehensive schema is the technique known as variable practice. For example, if you have problems with a particular move or type of move, you can set it up in a gym. Build up a schema by first doing an easy version over and over, pull-up style. Do it facing right and then left. Do it at various degrees of steepness. Change the holds around. Put the key hold slightly out of balance.

Pretty soon you will know when the move works and when it doesn't. You will also know what makes it fail sometimes and how to correct that. Is it a lack of flexibility? Then stretch the relevant joints and muscles. Is it strength?

Do some strength exercises. Is it pain? That, of course, is a real limit. Is it fear of the foot popping? Then do it on smaller and smaller footholds until you pop in a safe situation and develop confident judgment about the security of the footholds. This kind of practice is much more effective than blocked practice in which, for example, the same gym "routine" or well-known boulder circuit is done over and over until fatigue sets in.

Conclusions About Practicing For Skill

Many of the old debates about style and so-called ethics actually revolve around issues of learning. It should be clear now that hangdogging is the most efficient way to learn a new route. Traditional conventions such as lowering after a fall, not looking up, and not watching the climb get ascended represent obvious handicaps to learning. These handicaps used to lead to incredibly comical scenes of a person flowing effortlessly through multiple cruxes to a high point, then suddenly going all shaky and flailing off on relatively easy moves.

Learning is slow and difficult in states of exhaustion, fear, urgency, and lack of information. Oppositely, a fresh, relaxed, intelligent approach to learning new moves is most effective and efficient. It is best to practice new skills (develop solid schema) early in your training sessions and to hangdog when working routes that are hard for you.

Fitness Training For Climbing

The slack chain walk helps climbing balance.
Pull-ups and lat rows are the best climbing exercises.
Squats can help climbing a lot by teaching "total body power coordination."
The hang-board is a premiere way to develop practical finger endurance as are rubber donuts, manly spring-loaded grip exercises, etc.

These statements, all incorrect by the way, all raise the question about what kinds of training are valid for climbing. Obviously, all forms of climbing are valid training because they produce both improved skill and fitness. But how do you decide about other activities? Two ideas help clarify this problem. The idea of specificity (climbing-specific training) and transferability (the benefits gained by, say, weightlifting that might transfer to climbing).

The distinction between skill and fitness also helps to clarify this problem. The conclusions are: (1) Only climbing itself – call it "practice" – leads to improvement in skill. All other activities either have no effect or such a minor one as to make them a waste of time for purposes of climbing. (2) Fitness training leads to improvements in climbing only if it improves some element of fitness that is limiting performance or is needed to gain entry level for learning a new technique.

The "Training Effect"

A basic principle of exercise science is that adaptation occurs in exercise only in those parts or systems of the body that are stressed by the exercise. For example, running produces favorable adaptations in the legs, heart, and lungs (chest wall, actually), which improve the capacity for running. This is called the training effect. Systems not stressed show no adaptation. Even heroic amounts of running produce no favorable changes in the arms. The adaptations produced by running do transfer somewhat to other sports that depend on the same body parts and systems, for example, bicycle riding. Despite this, the effect is not immense.

In climbing you obviously need arm strength and endurance (especially in the grip), reasonable flexibility, minimal excess weight (either as fat or muscle in peripheral areas), and ordinary cardiovascular capacity and leg strength. So the effect of running on climbing would be expected to be small but positive, primarily by keeping fat down and maintaining cardiovascular fitness.

What about other exercises such as weight training? As it happens, weight training is highly specific. Isometric training of the biceps at one particular elbow position of say 90 degrees, transfers very poorly to isometric biceps strength at some other angle (say 60 degrees). Doing curls at one slow speed produces surprisingly little improvement in strength when doing them quickly. Grip strength shows a remarkable amount of specificity depending on the shape of the grip, the positions of the wrist and elbow, and the level of the muscles above the heart, kind of contraction, etc. Consequently, driving along in your car and squeezing a rubber donut is basically useless as climbing training.

Despite all of this, certain exercises that produce arm strength or endurance can help climbing performance. The specificity of strength training gives quite a few clues as to how it can best be done.

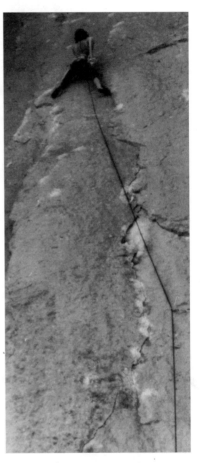

The late Wolfgang Güllich on "Powder in Your Eyes" (5.12c), Smith Rock, Oregon.

Climbing involves using muscles at different angles and in odd, sometimes contorted positions. These angles are seldom employed in standard body building style workouts, which involve repeating the same exact symmetrical, isolated movement over and over again.

For climbing, a frequent variation in exercise format is helpful, especially after basic competence and progress have been made at the standard exercises. Do pull-ups with wide grip, narrow grip, palms out, palms in, arms at different levels,

Eric Hörst on "Sweetest Taboo" (5.13a/b), NRG.

Rick Thompson photo

with one foot on a bench, etc. (This will perplex and sometimes annoy bodybuilding purists – just tell them you are using the "muscle confusion principle"!) Be cautious, though, not to exercise in uncomfortable or painful positions.

Squats are useless. They do nothing to improve climbing-specific fitness. Most people who can walk up stairs two steps at a time have all the leg strength needed for most rock climbs. There are also obvious weight concerns – few climbers would want to lug gigantic, bulging thighs up a cliff.

Whenever achieving a new grade, a burst of strength training seems to help even though the strength gained becomes unnecessary in many cases after consolidation of skill at that new level. Care must be taken not to glibly assume that problems arise from lack of strength. More often, they are due to inflexibility, lack of confidence (a feeling of strength is a great confidence-builder), or some more easily solved gap in technique.

Cross Training

The idea of cross training is obviously in conflict with these ideas of specificity. In fact, the only sports in which cross-training seems to be of practical help are the aerobic endurance sports, as popularized by the triathlon phenomenon. Of course, cross training can distract a climber from his or her primary sport and thereby promote health and reduce the risk of injury. It may also help to balance muscle development particularly of the "push muscles" in the shoulders and arms, which will reduce injury risk.

Fingerboard

As a final example, consider an analysis of the fingerboard. Using it in the traditional way – dangling from the handholds for a set length of time (x seconds or minutes, until exhaustion, etc.) – will not improve cardiovascular capacity. It will produce some increase in arm endurance and strength, but they will be somewhat specific to the particular holds and arm positions used. No benefits in flexibility will be expected, and overstretching of the elbows or shoulders may lead to injury.

Will it help skill? Obviously, you learned how to use the particular holds present on the board quite well. But the rest of your body is left unused and dangling in a position you should almost always avoid when climbing (ie. no weight on the feet.). A slight modification can make it more useful for training skill. Move your feet around on little holds back on a wall, and at the same time move your hands around on the board. All of this would ingrain a certain limited but useful kind of movement and position without detracting from the isometric strength and endurance-building functions of the device. Much more could be done, though, with an artificial wall, and the strength and endurance benefits are much more easily transferred to climbing on rock.

Of course, the fingerboard has other uses. It is a good warm-up device. It also helps maintain finger strength when you are unable to climb because it takes less exercise to maintain strength than to gain it.

Conclusion

So far, I have only discussed the most obvious and general ideas of Motor Learning as they apply to climbing. I do believe, however, that if you believe in and use this information it will empower you to achieve a higher level of performance.

Many other important concepts of motor skill and learning are waiting to be applied to climbing. Hints and tricks for even more efficient hangdogging can be found. As an example, is "backward chaining," – learning the climb in reverse (top-down) sequence – more efficient? Probably so! Should individual moves on a route be practiced in random order? Probably not. There are many other examples.

Despite this, there is no single best way to train or practice for any particular kind of climbing. It seems that as people learn any new skill, even babies learning how to walk, the brain generates numerous different solutions. These solutions are tried, the successful ones are retained, and the unsuccessful ones are discarded ("Neural Darwinism"). Original and creative solutions to problems of movement are routinely made as part of the learning process and will continue to be noticed and learned by others.

Until a certain point in time, the heel hook, the dyno, the back-step all simply did not exist and could not be learned. Somebody or perhaps many people created them in the course of learning to climb, and now these moves are commonplace. It is important to keep an open mind and a willingness to learn, especially from people new to the sport and those brave enough to try to change it.

Quick Guide to Training	Cardiovascular	Anaerobic Capacity	Local Endurance	Local Strength	Flexibility	Skill	Body Composition	Risk of Injury
Total Body Aerobic	++	$0^{20.}$	+	-/$0^{9.}$	0	0^{3}	++	Ø
Leg Aerobic	+	$0^{20.}$	0	-/$0^{10.}$	$-^{2.}$	$0^{3.}$	+	Ø
Arm Aerobic	$0^{1.}$	$0^{20.}$	+	-/$0^{9.}$	0	$0^{3.}$	+	Ø
Fingerboard	0	+	+	++	0	$0/+^{4.}$	0	±
Campusing	0	++	0/+	++	0	$0/+^{23.}$	0	$±^{21.}$
Bouldering[11.]	0	++	+	+	0	++	0	$±^{5.}$
Artificial Walls	0/+	+	++	+	0/+	$++^{12.}$	0	$±^{5.}$
Top Ropes	0/+	+	++	+	0	++	0	$±^{5.}$
Laps on Climb	0/+	+	++	+	0	+	+	$±^{5.}$
Hangdog	0	+	0/+	0/+	0	$++^{16.}$	0	$Ø^{6.}$
Traditional Style	0	+	0/+	0	0	$+^{16.}$	0	±±
Weights	0	0/+	+	++	$0/+^{13.}$	$0^{7.}$	$-^{7.}$	$Ø^{7.}$
Stretching	0	0	0	0	++	+	0	Ø
Slack Chain &	0	0	0	0	0	$0/+^{8.}$	0	0
Tricks	0	0	0	0/+	0	$0^{8.}$	0	±
Visualization	0	0	0	0	0	+	0	0
Dieting[14.]	Var	0/-	-	-	0	0	+/-	±
Intervals:[17.] Total Body	0/+	++	+	+	0	0	0	$±^{19.}$
Intervals:[18.] Arms	0	+	+	+	0	0	0	$±^{19.}$
Eccentric Exercise Upper Body	0	0/+	0/+	$++^{22.}$	0	0	0	$±±^{21.}$

++ = Very favorable
+ = Favorable
0 = No effect
- = Adverse effect

Ø = Decreased risk of overuse injury
± = Increased risk of overuse injury
Var = Variable

Guide to Training – Footnotes

[1] Arm muscles are unable to produce significant cardiovascular training stress. May be able to do so in very heavily muscled individuals.

[2] Running, cycling, etc., all lead to stiffness unless done with stretching before and after.

[3] Aerobic exercise: Repetitive, programmed, does not contribute to motor programs used in climbing.

[4] Fingerboards involve use of muscles of upper extremities in ways rarely found in climbing, i.e. no foot contact. If used with foot contact, could contribute some, although absence of movement would still be a disadvantage.

[5] All simulation exercises carry risk of overuse if combined with too much climbing or done too often.

[6] Hangdogging is better for avoiding injury.

[7] Weight lifting may encourage bad technique (see text) and may lead to excessive muscle weight. Weight training of antagonists can decrease risk of injury.

[8] Slight positive benefit possible, but not worth the time.

[9] Extreme endurance training can lead to losses of strength in the muscles used. Decreases fiber size.

[10] Running alone can lead to atrophy of the arms (e.g., marathon runners). Unlikely to do so in person who also does some upper extremity strength exercises.

[11] Depends on kind of bouldering. Bouldering can simulate almost any kind of climbing, e.g., circuits.

[12] Artificial walls are somewhat different from natural rock. Skill transfer is less.

[13] Weight lifting done through full range of motion can increase flexibility. Bulky muscles can limit range of motion.

[14] Caloric restriction dieting, fat loss regimen.

[15] Low body fat, adequate muscle mass in climbing-related muscles.

[16] Traditional style sharpens skills of reading rock ("perception"), making decisions and planning a sequence ("information processing"). Hangdogging sharpens the physical skills of execution of moves and speeds up the learning of very hard climbs or sequences, thereby avoiding injury.

[17] For example, using a Versaclimber at high resistance or tilted backward, intervals in cross-country skiing, etc.

[18] For example, Frenchies or the Enduro-Master at high resistance, etc.

[19] Very high intensity effort. Risky.

[20] At high level of intensity (90 - 100% mVO2) may produce improved lactic acid tolerance and so improve anaerobic capacity. Can also help with "mental toughness" at this level of intensity.

[21] Markedly risky except for the highly trained individual. Only do once or twice per week.

[22] Also adds strength to soft tissue supports, tendons, ligaments, etc. if done properly.

[23] Positive benefit for overhanging routes with deadpoint or dynamic moves.

Strength Training

The only way to discover the limits of the possible is to go beyond them into the impossible.

Arthur C. Clarke

O.K., here it is! What everybody wants. The chapter on strength training. Yes, it will help you get stronger, but it won't necessarily help you climb better. If you don't understand this statement, then please go back and read Chapter 1.

The thirteen articles contained in this chapter will expose you to both strength-training exercises and training approaches. Read each of them thoroughly; however, be objective in deciding which one(s) is most relevant to you at your climbing ability.

Try to avoid the natural tendency to focus only on the articles that contain new and exciting gym exercises, such as those in the *Super Recruiting* article. The most powerful pieces in this chapter may very well be Todd Skinner's look into *Training At the Crags* and Mike Pont's *Indoor Climbing*. Also, don't miss the last two articles on Sportsmassage and Stretching. They contain training techniques you'll want to begin putting to use today!

Finally, pay special attention to the first article, *Breaking The Ties That Bind*. It will help you determine if more strength training is actually what you need. Arguably, the majority of climbers would profit more from an increased focus on rock technique and mental training, than from a new strength-training regimen. Strength is important to climbing, but time invested in improving technique and mental control will pay faster and greater dividends.

BREAKING THE TIES THAT BIND

The pursuit of peak performance starts with getting to know your patterns at the crags, in the gym, and in life in general. You must become aware of your climbing-related strengths, weaknesses, and desires, for without this knowledge you will ultimately lack the power to succeed.

It will be quite easy to identify your strengths because it's human nature to think about and practice the things at which we are good. Because of this, I believe that your strengths are really your weaknesses because they consume the time and energy you should be focusing elsewhere.

(page opposite)
Amy Whistler on "When I Was A Young Girl, I Had Me A Cowboy" (5.13), Wild Iris Wall, Wyoming.

Lisa Hörst crankin' "Exoduster" (5.10b), New River Gorge, West Virginia.

Consequently, identifying your weaknesses will require a paradigm shift – a dramatic change in the way you "see" yourself. You must then break with tradition and focus your work on these weaknesses. Only then will you ever approach your true potential.

Too many climbers, myself included, have wasted precious years practicing and training the things at which they already excel, while the "ball and chain" of their weaknesses unknowingly holds them down. So identify your weaknesses and break the ties that bind!

Asking The Right Questions

The best way to identify your weaknesses is to ask yourself a series of detailed questions. To identify your physical and technical weaknesses begin by asking things like: do I fail on a route because my biceps pump out, or do my forearms go first? Does my footwork deteriorate when times get tough? Do I climb too slowly and get caught in the paralysis of analysis? Do I lack the flexibility to step onto the holds I need? Do I over grip the rock when I become anxious? Do I lack the strength to power off small holds? Am I carrying too much fat to escape the force of gravity? Are my muscles the right size for the beach, but too big and heavy for climbing steep routes?

Some questions for identifying mental errors are: do I fail to see the sequence, or do I fail to try something new when the obvious doesn't work? Do I sabotage myself before I leave the ground by thinking about the "negatives" that might affect me? Do I try too hard or not hard enough? Am I aware of what I tell myself when the situation gets tough? Do I turn negatives into positives, or do I become the "King of Pain"?

Three Steps To Success

Now that you're aware of some of your weaknesses you can begin to turn them into strengths with the following procedures:

- Know your outcome – Write down, then regularly visualize what you want to achieve. Belief gives birth to reality.
- Take action – Nothing worth having comes without a little work, pain, and risk. Get started today!
- Have sensory acuity – Are the actions you are taking producing the desired results? If not, modify or change your approach.

Step three is critical. It is all too common to get locked into workouts or climbing routines that are no longer effective. Have you become trapped in the same workout ritual, or do you climb at the same area over and over? If so, you are cheating yourself. You must be dynamic and take chances!

Commitment and Desire: The Equalizers

Finally, you must review your level of commitment. Given your current skill level, are your desire and commitment strong enough to send you towards your goals? If not, you must either increase your commitment or lower your goals. Hopefully, you will choose the former and decide to flash!

DESIGN A STRENGTH PROGRAM

In recent years, perhaps no sport has experienced as dramatic an increase in athletic performance as rock climbing. Today's average climber is capable of a standard that a mere decade ago only a few climbers achieved, and the number of people climbing at extreme levels is growing quickly.

There are many reasons for these improvements, including sticky-soled shoes, sport climbing tactics, and, particularly significant, the fact that many people are pushing themselves in the gym as well as on the rock. In climbing, however, unlike most other sports, there is a limited amount of information to direct people in the safest and most effective ways to train, a fact reflected in the large number of climbers injured by improper workouts or on the rock.

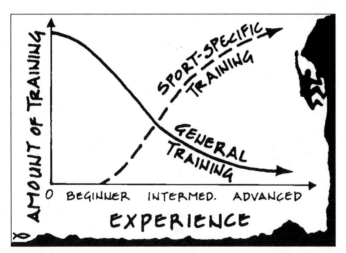

How To Train

In training for any sport there are two aspects to be addressed: general (multilateral) development and specialized training. The workouts of both novice and advanced climbers will include both these aspects but in different proportions.

The beginner's workout will consist of mainly general exercises such as circuit training (upper and lower body), aerobic activity such as running, and flexibility exercises, leading to a solid physical base. These workouts should be designed to improve your all-around muscular strength and endurance, as well as ligament and tendon tolerance. Although the novice can perform a limited number of specific exercises, emphasis must remain on well-balanced development before starting on highly-specialized sport-specific exercises like the hangboard, campus board, and the like.

An intermediate climber might spend about half of his training time on specific exercises designed to mimic the extreme movements and positions of a difficult climb, building toward a majority of such exercises with time. The body then responds through adaptations of the central nervous system, connective tissues, and muscles. Spend a lot of time focusing on the workhorse "pull muscles" – back, biceps, forearms – to increase both pure strength and endurance. Unfortunately, these exercises can easily cause injury, particularly to tendons. Add them gradually and perform them only after a complete warm-up.

Each person, regardless of skill level, must train according to his needs, abilities, limitations or injuries, potential, and desire. In developing an individualized program, evaluate both your climbing strengths and weaknesses (you might ask a friend for an objective view). If you are normally limited by technique and not strength, you need more time on the rock rather than in the gym. If your technique exceeds your physical abilities, then you need specific gym training.

In evaluating your physical parameters, don't qualify yourself against your peers because individual strengths and weaknesses, body fat percentage, flexibility, "pull muscle" power and endurance, and antagonistic muscle conditioning vary widely in their translation to real climbing ability. Instead, focus on the barriers that the lack of physical conditioning impose on your climbing.

Goal Setting

Goal setting is a strong motivator for training. Be specific with dates and events such as "20 pull-ups by December 1st," or "lose 10 pounds by February 1st." Make a list of specific climbs or climbing goals as well.

Planning

Workout schedules can be difficult to plan and often even harder to stick to. However, a written "game plan" is essential for anyone serious about training. Map out the quantity and order of exercises for a particular workout, your workout schedule for a particular week, and a long-range plan.

Daily Workouts

A complete warm-up is of paramount importance before you work out or climb. Start with a short general warm-up of light running, biking or skipping rope, then stretch the body parts about to be trained. If some bouldering is on the agenda, do that before the gym exercises so the muscles and mind are fresh. This is critical so your technique can be true to form; it also makes the session more enjoyable. Once you are in the gym, begin with general exercises so as to be completely warmed up for the more stressful specifics.

For sport-specific exercises, start with those that build pure strength (exercises that produce muscle failure in less than 20 seconds), and move on to the more fatiguing endurance builders (failure in 20 seconds to two minutes). Finish with the smaller muscles; the forearms, for example. Spend the final minutes of the workout session doing some sort of cool-down activity, such as stretching.

Weekly Schedule

A weekly workout schedule may seem unnecessary, especially if you're one of those training fanatics who go to the gym on a daily basis, however, many workout regimens are less productive than they could be. Plan your workout frequency carefully, remembering that rest and recovery time are as critical as the workouts themselves.

During and following a workout your body goes through many changes. Workout stimulus must occur at the right frequency to obtain the maximum training effect. If you are climbing a lot, you may limit the number of days in the gym to one. For weekend climbers, two days of strength training a week is generally best. In a pure training phase such as winter, the typical climber would get the best gains from three evenly spaced workouts, four for an advanced climber.

Plan workouts to allow your body just enough time to regenerate in between sessions. In most cases this recovery period is about 48 hours, although it can vary between 24 and 72 hours depending on genetics, workout intensity, diet and quality of rest time. In any case, accurately spaced (for you), consistently performed workouts will provide the most significant progress.

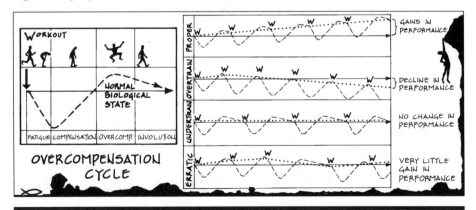

Performing workouts too frequently or overtraining can cause injuries and a loss of strength.

Too much off time between workouts will also limit growth. For most, a break of more than 72 hours between sessions makes the training program a maintenance regimen at best.

Finally, even the most disciplined of us can find our workouts becoming erratic. You might do several good, well-spaced workouts, then for one reason or another spend a period away from the gym. Such an on-and-off schedule usually results in little if any strength gain.

Periodization

Everyone from beginner to world-class competitor goes through a performance cycle during the course of a year. Many people experience periods when they feel physically and mentally honed, when their level of performance has peaked.

For a competitive climber, this peak period should coincide with a major contest; you can also manipulate your schedule to provide several peaks during the course of the year. Non-competitive climbers also like to peak, but their "competition" may be a road trip.

A three-phase cycle can enable you to plan out a peak using "periodization." The phases are preparatory, competition, and transition. Using a calendar already marked with major trips or competitions, you can lay out a yearly plan.

The preparatory phase generally commences during the off-season and mostly involves increasing amounts of gym training and bouldering. As the on-season (competitive phase) nears, you make a gradual shift onto the rock. During this phase, attempt to maintain your level of gym training. As the trip or competition nears, taper off your strength training time to focus on climbing. Most persons will peak soon after this taper begins.

The length of an athlete's peak can vary greatly from one individual to the next. The peak state should be followed by a transition period of less intense training and performance.

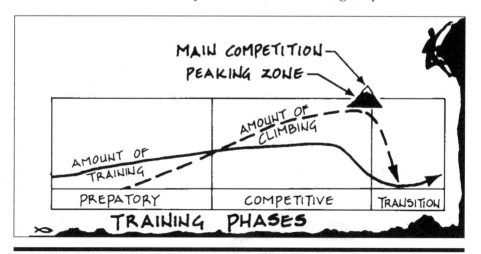

Upon completion of a long trip or important competition, rest for ten to 30 days before resuming light training or climbing. Many athletes use the transition phase to participate in other activities (active rest). This is also the time to get rid of the accumulated aches and pains of the past cycle or season. Most commonly, this phase consumes the first half of the off-season, before beginning the next cycle's preparatory phase.

BASIC TRAINING PROGRAM

This training article is appropriate for people just entering the sport or those with up to a few years of experience. Clearly, each individual progresses at a different rate depending on time, motivation, level of "base" fitness, and genetics. Some may outgrow this program in six months while it may suit others for many years.

Training programs for climbing may be more complex than for most other sports. Whereas you may think you simply need to begin a regimen of pull-ups and finger work-outs, the road to peak performance on the rock requires a holistic approach.

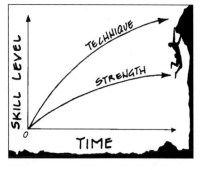

A good training program for climbing includes items such as bouldering to learn problem solving, logging lots of distance on routes at many different areas to learn technique, and stretching to become flexible. Also important is honing your diet for maximum energy and minimum body fat, developing mental control, resting sufficiently to avoid injury, regularly evaluating yourself to determine your current weaknesses, and performing various strength-training exercises specific to climbing movements.

During your first few years in the sport, the focus of your training program should be placed on the first few items listed above. Improvements in problem solving, technique, diet, and mental control can have an overnight effect on your climbing ability. Progress on the rock will be rapid and dead obvious if you follow this advice.

Conversely, the results of sport-specific strength training come painfully slow for most and are not the priority for novice climbers. Too much strength training early in your climbing career may not only stunt your technical growth but will often result in injuries.

A focused effort on training early on may not only stunt your technical growth but will often result in injuries that can drag on for months or years.

I will touch on the key elements of a beginner's program. It is by no means comprehensive and should be modified and supplemented as you improve and as new information becomes available. Maybe the most basic training principle of all is that your program must be progressive. So keep it fresh, and change it as your skill level increases.

Training Technique

Climb a lot, plain and simple. Two to four days per week is best. As mentioned earlier, it's important to gain experience on many different types of rock. Hit your local bouldering spots and climbing gym during the week, then travel to more distant crags on weekends. This will maximize your learning curve.

If you don't have a nearby crag or gym, then invest in building a small home gym. The couple hundred dollars you spend (go in on it with a few friends) can be the best investment you make in your future climbing ability.

Be observant of other climbers' techniques. Spend your rest time at the gym and crags studying the positions, movements, and attack of expert climbers, then model them when it's your turn to climb. It doesn't matter if they're climbing 5.12 and you're climbing 5.6. The basics are the same: weight the feet as much as possible, conserve energy, find good rest positions, and be aggressive –climbing fast – when the rock gets steep.

Remember, your technique can never be too good. So practice, practice, practice!

Training Strength

Beginning climbers probably get all the sport-specific training they need from the prescribed two to four days per week of climbing.

I suggest you perform a few supplemental exercises for the antagonistic (opposing) muscles to prevent the muscle-imbalance injuries so common to climbers. The antagonists include the pectorals (chest), deltoids (shoulder), triceps (back of the upper arm), and finger extensors (top of the forearms). As far as sets and frequency are concerned, try for two sets, two days per week. The weight should be moderate – enough to allow you 20 reps per set. Most importantly, ignore any advice to use heavy weights, lower reps, and more sets. That sort of regimen is for bodybuilders in search of mass, NOT for climbers!

A Smith Rock, Oregon, classic – "Latest Rage" (5.12b).

If you are not climbing much, add a limited amount of "climbing exercises": five sets of pull-ups, five sets of abdominal crunches, three sets of dips, and a few sets of straight-arm hangs – all done to muscular failure. For the first year or two forget fingerboard training or any other super-specific, super-stressful exercises. Also, just say no to bicep curls unless you're planning on spending more time at the beach than the crags!

Concerning leg exercises and aerobic workouts, you should do none and some, respectively. No serious climber would ever want to do any exercises designed to increase leg muscle mass. This means forget any leg extensions, curls, or squats, except in rehabilitation applications. Moderate amounts of aerobic exercise, along with regular climbing, will give you all the leg exercise you need.

Regularly performed aerobic exercise will also improve your overall fitness and help burn extra calories. Running is probably best because it burns more calories than most other activities and reduces leg size for some persons. Try for two to four 20- to 30-minute runs per week. If you do more, the resultant fatigue may interfere with your climbing.

Other Areas of Concern

In addition to training technique and strength, you must focus on improving mental control and your diet/body weight.

As you begin lead climbing, you'll find your mental capabilities may be more limiting than the physical. Relaxation, poise, and control are of paramount importance in our sport, and they are all managed by the mind. Read the chapter on Mental Training a few times and make a focused effort to apply the information each time you climb.

The subjects of diet and body weight are too complex to get into here in much depth. But remember, it's strength-to-weight ratio that matters in climbing, not pure strength. Nearly every climber I know (myself included) could have more productive dietary habits. It could be argued that even the best, most intense workout is negated if it's followed by a heap of junk food and beer!

For now I suggest that you carefully study Chapter 5 about diet and nutrition. Focus daily on improving the quality of the food you consume. Positive, permanent changes take time, and by all means don't ever crash diet.

Finally, I should mention the importance of goals. They are what fuel the action and maintain the discipline needed to progress in this sport. Always have a running list of climbs to tick and areas to visit. Remember, a goal is simply a dream put on paper. Only then do most people take the necessary action to make it reality.

ADVANCED TRAINING PROGRAM

This advanced training program could be called a smart, holistic approach to getting ahead of the Joneses and staying uninjured. It is designed for persons with extensive climbing experience and a significant base-fitness level. As with the Basic Program detailed earlier, this information can only point you in the direction of the best performance gains to be realized for someone of your ability. Time and experience will help you hone the regimen into the best program for you! A final word of caution: if your top climbing level is less than 5.10/5.11, then the Basic Training Program is probably more appropriate and safer for you at this time.

The better you become, the greater your desire to improve. Unfortunately, the better you get at difficult routes, the more difficult it gets to improve!

Sound complex? Not nearly as complex as developing a holistic training program for an advanced climber. To reach the upper echelon in our sport, you must have the dedication and focus to work on the many things that affect climbing performance. Unfortunately, many dedicated climbers' singular focus is strength training. More strength is good, but it's only one piece of the puzzle.

Tony Yaniro on "Babalouie" (5.12c), Wild Iris Wall, Wyoming.

Mike McGill photo

Identify Your Weaknesses

The quickest way to identify your true weakness is to ask yourself questions. Does my footwork deteriorate when times get tough? Do I get anxious and tight as I head into the crux? Do my forearms balloon before I reach the top? Do I blow sequences I know by heart?

Ask yourself a slew of questions along these lines on a weekly basis. This will help you identify where your training time is best spent. Then write down and visualize these training goals, and take some action each and every day to make them become reality. Finally, check back about once a month to determine if these actions are producing the desired results? If not, change your approach! You may not be training your true weaknesses.

The Mind – Weakest Link In the Chain?

I am a firm believer that the most important muscle for climbing is between your ears. A whole book would be needed to discuss the thousands of ways your mind affects climbing performance. However, the Mental Training chapter will have to do for now.

Ponder this: mental training is the quickest means for you, the advanced climber, to improve your performance! This means using your mind to improve the efficiency of your actions both on and off the rock.

A microscopic sample of mental exercises could include:
• Improvements in studying and visualizing sequences
• Eliminating pressure or learning how to use it to your benefit
• Controlling your emotions
• Experimenting to find the best pre- and post-performance rituals for you
• Learning how subtle changes in your diet affect your energy levels
• Determining the perfect amount of warm-up before a big redpoint attempt
• Knowing how to get really motivated
• Learning how to read your body, adjust your workouts, and avoid injury.

Let's face it – we all have a lot of homework to do in this area.

Strength Training

If you are an advanced climber, you probably do a lot of strength training already. So let's start by asking a few questions. Are the exercises you perform effective? Do they produce noticeable results on the rock? Do they help you through performance plateaus? Are they low-stress exercises? Do they produce muscle soreness but never tendon or joint pain? Do you still spend more time climbing than strength training?

If you've answered one or more of these questions with a "no," then let's talk! Most exceptionally fit climbers agree that noticeable gains in strength take a long time. They are achieved in terms of months and years. Unfortunately, climbers as a breed want Ben Moon-like finger strength tomorrow. They go overboard on strength-training exercises and thus increase their risk of overtraining-type injuries.

A better approach would involve more focus on fine tuning technique and the mind, along with a moderate amount of strength-training exercises. Remember, improvements in technique and the mental "game" CAN come overnight. So more attention paid in these areas might result in immediate gains in apparent strength! Better footwork and more poise conserve energy. You haven't made the gas tank bigger, but you've improved the miles per gallon.

Sure it would be nice to make the engine stronger, too. So here are some basic guidelines for your strength-training sessions.

Forget about pull-ups! The key pull muscle skill on hard routes is the ability to lock-off. Work one-arm lock-offs once or twice a week. Go bouldering more often to develop power and focus. For pull-muscle endurance chalk-up lots of mileage on routes near the top of your ability level, either on real rock or in the gym, and do a few sets of Frenchies weekly.

The Fingers

Fingers take time and patience! Get injured, and you might miss a month or season of climbing. Two rules to minimize your chances of finger injuries are to weight your fingers no more than four days per week, and to always use preventative taping at the base of the middle two fingers when seriously training or attempting stressful routes.

The most common climbing/training schedule for advanced climbers is two days on, one day off, two days on, two days off. Always do your climbing, bouldering, or plastic workout first while the muscles and nervous system are fresh. Finish your session with the supplemental strength exercises you have planned.

Mike Freeman cranking some thin, powerful finger moves on "Model Obsession" (5.12c), Sex Wall, Pennsylvania.

For power, bouldering is king. So get to your gym or local bouldering spot at least twice per week. Effective gym exercises for training power include heavy finger rolls, campusing, and some super-recruiting on the fingerboard. Perform these exercises no more than twice per week.

Also important is "Power Endurance" – the ability to do many hard moves in a row, despite an ever-growing muscular burn. This training is painful in the sense that your muscles will be screaming, and the Gumby in your mind will be saying, "let go!" Part of developing power endurance is mental: the ability to hang on through more hard moves while telling yourself there's a bit of a rest just ahead – even if there isn't.

Work laps, trying to climb up and down, on pumpy routes you have wired at your local crag or gym. The perfect route would be steep with comfortable, non-stressful holds and would contain a few cruxes separated by more moderately difficult sections. At your gym you CAN design the perfect route. Do it! The right route for you is one where you can hang on for 5 to 15 minutes. You should be climbing pretty much continuously throughout this time, but work effective shake-outs (G-tox) between crux sections.

When your forearms are frying and your grip is no more, you'll want to drink some water and then relax for 15 to 30 minutes. Well-conditioned climbers will be able to work several of these burns during the course of a workout.

Wrap-up

As with any training program it's imperative to work into it gradually. Injuries are so unforgiving! Reduce the frequency of the above exercises if you ever begin to experience any shoulder or elbow pain. Replace them with a few push-muscle exercises (as discussed in the Basic Training Program) in case a muscle imbalance is the culprit in developing your injury.

Drink lots of water or sports drink throughout your workout. Dehydration decreases coordination and strength and increases your chance of injury. After your workout eat a good meal with lots of carbos and some protein, so your body can rebuild and refuel. A good night's sleep finishes out your perfect workout.

Most importantly, listen to your body, and adjust your routine accordingly. Forget the specifics of the local rock star's training program, and develop the best workout program for you.

PULL-MUSCLE EXERCISES

Pull-ups and the Bachar Ladder are now synonymous with pull-muscle training for climbing. Unfortunately, the standard pull-up is overrated as a strength builder, and the Bachar Ladder's injury record is frightening. There are alternatives, though.

Much of the specific upper-body training for climbing centers on the big muscles used in pulling: the back, shoulders, and upper arms. This article will focus on these "pull" muscles. Our link to the rock – the forearms and hands – will be discussed later in this chapter.

Theory

To understand how to best train these muscles, it would help to understand the energy processes enabling movement. In climbing, energy production in the "pull" muscles most often comes from the ATP-CP system (ATP and CP are high-energy phosphate compounds that are common to all muscle cells in small amounts) and the lactic acid system.

The ATP-CP system provides rapid energy releases for brief intense movements such as a vigorous boulder problem or a one-arm pull-up. Consequently, it must be on call for the most powerful moves of a climb. Training it involves brief sets of intense effort – five to 15 seconds – separated by relatively long rests of at least two minutes. This regimen may seem surprisingly easy, but it really is the best rate of stimulus for producing gains in power.

The lactic acid system produces energy much differently. In our sport the majority of motions rely on this process' function, a major factor in whether you have enough endurance to finish a long pitch.

Carbohydrates in the form of glycogen fuel the lactic acid system, which can operate in either the presence or absence of oxygen. Initially, the procedure runs with oxygen, yielding steady energy and only gradual fatigue. As work intensity increases, however, your lungs and heart fail to provide enough oxygen to the muscles, forcing creation of energy at the expense of lactic acid production. The resulting accumulation of lactic acid leads to fatigue and then muscle failure. This cycle is yet another good reason to do some cardiovascular training and quit smoking, considering that a strong heart and lungs will allow the muscles to work at a slightly higher intensity level without lactic acid build up.

The best regimen to train this system involves moderate-intensity exercises performed for an extended period of time. Sets lasting between 20 seconds and two minutes are ideal, with rests between sets of at least two minutes.

Just Doing It

The only absolutely necessary part of a workout is a warm-up. Begin with a general warm-up of five to ten minutes of running, biking, or a similar activity. Move on to some upper-body stretches, finishing with several short sets of pull-ups. The warm-up ideally ends at an intensity close to that of the first set of power exercises. Perform all the power exercises before beginning on the more fatiguing endurance builders.

Described herein are a number of excellent "pull" exercises. Some build power, others endurance. It's important to note that what may be a power exercise for one person might be an endurance promoter for another. As a general rule, an exercise causing muscular failure in 15 seconds or less develop power; the others improve endurance.

Since body weight is the resistance for most of these exercises, the use of an elastic bungee cord or a counterweight system will enable you to manipulate the length of time until failure. Standing in several loops of bungee cord will turn a power-building exercise into endurance. Conversely, you might want to add weight to your harness to turn regular pull-ups into power builders.

The Exercises

Uneven Grip Pull-ups

Put one hand on the bar, the other between six and 18 inches lower, holding on to a towel looped over the bar or with two or three fingers through a loop of webbing. Both hands will pull, with the upper hand emphasized – this will help develop one-arm power! Do each set to failure, then switch arms. As you get stronger, increase the length of the loop. In a few months to a year you'll be able to do a one-arm pull-up.

One-arm Lock-offs

Start with a regular two-arm chin-up (palms towards you), lock-off on one arm, and let go with the other. Hold the lock-off with your chin above the bar as long as you can, then lower slowly. Don't let yourself go down fast! Jump down and shake out, then do the other arm. If you can't hold these, start with the aid of a bungee cord or hold on with one finger of the other hand. (See One-arm Lock-off article later in this chapter for a more detailed discussion.)

One-arm Statics

These are much like the one-arm lock-offs except they're done palms away and at angles of 30, 90, and 120 degrees. Pull up with two arms until you reach the desired angle. Let go with one hand and hold static as long as possible. Shake out and switch arms. Very hard, best for advanced persons.

Weighted Pull-ups/Heavy Lat-Pulldowns

The easiest way to do these is on a lat-pull-down machine. Load on a lot of weight and do palms away pulldowns, pulling the bar below your chin. The alternate way is to do weighted pull-ups. Add as much weight around your waist as you need so that you can do only between three and six reps. Excellent power builders!

Pull muscle exercises. (top) One-arm lock-off and uneven-grip pull-up. (bottom) Lat pulldown and weighted pull-up.

(left) The Typewriter and (right) Frenchies.

Typewriters

Grip the bar palms away with the distance between your hands equal to about half your height. Pull-up and immediately move to the right until your right hand touches the side of your chest. Hold there in a lock-off for three seconds, then move back left until your left hand touches your chest. Hold that lock for three seconds, then move back right. Continue in this way until your chin drops below the bar. Beginners may want to use a bungee.

Frenchies

Start at the top position of a pull-up (palms away and hands shoulder width apart) and hold there in a two-arm lock-off for seven seconds. Pull-up again; however, this time you'll lower half way and lock-off at 90 degree for seven seconds. Do another pull-up but lower and lock-off at about 120 degrees for seven seconds. Perform this exact sequence and you've completed one full cycle.

Do as many cycles as possible without stopping or cheating until muscular failure – this represents one set. Record the number of cycles you achieve per set.

Beware! Frenchies are hard, as well as quite grueling; however, they are great endurance builders and they strengthen your lock-off ability at the multiple angles. Use bungees to start if you can't do at least two full cycles.

30 Second Pull-ups

These are regular pull-ups performed in slow motion. Take 10 seconds to go up, and come down to a slow count of 20. Continue until you can't perform the exercise according to these guidelines.

A PERSONALIZED PROGRAM

You now know the exercises; your next question is how many sets of each? The exact formula is different for everyone, but one common principle is variety. By regularly changing the three or four exercises you choose, you'll greatly reduce the chance of injury. The actual volume of exercises depends on many factors including physical condition, history of injury, goals, and time. With this in mind, here are general guidelines for the total number of sets per pull-muscle workout:

	Power Sets	Endurance Sets
Beginner		
(< 1 year of training)	2 - 3 sets	2 - 3 sets
Intermediate		
(1 - 3 years. of training)	3 - 6 sets	3 - 5 sets
Advanced		
(> 3 years. of training)	6 - 12 sets	5 - 8 sets

The author sending
"Wonderama"
(5.12a/b), at Safe
Harbor, Pennsylvania.

John Dine photo

Pull-up Intervals

This is an exercise I designed to accustom the pull muscles to working during periods of high blood acidity (low pH). On long sustained climbs, lactic acid buildup increases blood acidity, partially contributing to the burn and tightness prior to complete muscle failure.

Each pull-up interval is a minute long (use a stop watch to time exactly) consisting of a number of pull-ups in a row to start the minute, followed by a rest and shake-out for the remainder of that minute.

Start with a set of four pull-ups (this will take about 10 seconds) then jump down and rest for the next 50 seconds. When that minute is up, start the next set of 4 pull-ups, followed by a rest for the remainder. Continue in this fashion until you can no longer do the prescribed number of pull-ups. If you make it to 20 minutes, 80 total pull-ups, then increase the sets to 5 reps next time.

The Standard Pull-up

The old standby...do it on anything you can hold on to. Vary the width of your grip from set to set. Palms away is best; always go until failure.

All the Rest

So what about all the other exercises that work the "pull" muscles? As a general rule, avoid isolation exercises like bicep curls and lat pullovers because they train the muscles in a way that they will never be used on a climb. Even worse, exercises like these tend to greatly increase muscle size, a quality that is best avoided. The Bachar Ladder and rope climbing are good exercises if you are strong enough to do them in control and mentally disciplined enough not to overuse them. These are best left to advanced persons!

These exercises make up only half of a great workout. The other half involves quality rest time as discussed earlier and, of course, good nutrition. Always take it easy when starting a new training regimen, then gradually increase the volume with time.

Also, don't forget to do some training for the antagonistic "push" muscles to promote muscle balance. Remember that pain doesn't always mean gain, so cut back immediately if you feel any unusual pangs.

THE ONE-ARM LOCK-OFF REVISITED

The standard pull-up has long been the staple exercise for climbers. Several sets of pull-ups performed three or four days a week will provide most climbers with the necessary "pull-muscle" strength to progress into the mid grades in the course of a few months to a year.

Unfortunately, the standard pull-up may not provide the more specialized types of pull-muscle strength needed for more difficult routes. We all know climbers who can knock off a decent number of pull-ups (greater than 15 or 20) but cannot regularly knock off 5.10s or 5.11s! Although poor technique is likely the problem for some, many lack the important skill of being able to fully lock-off on a hold with one hand while making the reach to the next finger hold or good jam with the other.

This lock-off skill is especially critical as the distance between holds and the angle of the rock increase. For these reasons, intermediate and advanced climbers would be well served to add the one-arm lock-off exercise to their training "menu." In fact, connoisseurs of overhanging rock may want to make the one-arm lock-off one of their new staple exercises.

> ### ONE-ARM LOCK-OFF TIPS
>
> • Focus on pulling the bar toward your armpit.
>
> • Lift your knees to waist height while in the lock-off.
>
> • Try to keep breathing while holding a lock-off.
>
> • If at first you have difficulty holding the lock-off, stand in a loop of bungee cord or use one finger of the other hand.
>
> • Do not work this exercise on a fingerboard.

Doing Them

As a general rule, you should not train the one-arm lock-off exercise unless your "one-set-max" number of pull-ups is at least 15. Until then, continue to work four to eight sets of pull-ups (palms away) per workout with two- to four-minute rest between sets until you reach this criteria.

For the able and ready, let me first make two important points.

• One-arm lock-offs are a high-intensity exercise that requires a sharp focus and reasonably fresh muscles.

• This exercise is quite stressful and could result in injury if overtrained or done improperly.

Perform the lock-offs early in your workout while the mind and body are fresh. A thorough upper body warm-up is mandatory.

For your warm-up begin with some stretches for the arms, shoulders, and back, as well as several sets of standard pull-ups. A few minutes of sportsmassage performed on the upper arms and back is beneficial.

Begin with a regular chin-up (palms toward you). Lock off completely at the top on one arm, and let go with the other. Hold the lock-off with your chin above the bar as long as you can, all the while focusing on pulling the bar "under your armpit." When you begin to lose the lock, either grab back on with the other hand, or lower slowly, which is tougher. Don't let yourself down fast! Jump down and gather yourself briefly, then do the other arm. Perform three to five sets for each side with a few minutes of rest between sets.

If you can't hold these at first, do them by holding on with one finger of the other hand or by standing in a loop of bungee cord. In a short time you'll be holding a true one-arm lock-off for ten or twenty seconds!

(top) Regular one-arm lock off.

(bottom) Same exercise with a "helper finger."

Advanced Lock-offs

There are two harder "variations" you can begin to work when you are able to perform five sets of 20-second lock-offs.

Variation 1

Variation 1 is the same lock-off exercise except with your palms facing away (pull-up position). This is a bit harder because you receive less help from the bicep, but it is more sport specific and thus more useful! Do two sets of lock-offs the regular way, then do three more sets in this new position. Again, try to build up to 20 seconds per set.

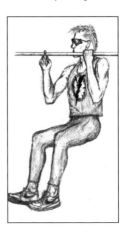

Variation 2

Variation 2 involves performing the lock-offs below the bar at "arm-angles" of 45, 90, and 120 degrees. Pull up with two arms until you reach the desired angle. Let go with one hand and hold static as long as possible. These are very difficult and should be done only when you can successfully do Variation 1.

AN OVERVIEW OF FINGER TRAINING

The fingers/forearms are often the point of muscular failure when climbing, thus making them the focus of many training programs. Unfortunately, the combined stress of climbing and training can easily result in injuries or even acute trauma. Indeed, there are few active advanced climbers who have not experienced tendon or joint problems in their fingers at one time or another.

The most obvious and simple way to avoid such strains is to eliminate all finger training outside of actual climbing itself. However, this is not an option for many of today's climbers who have sentenced themselves to penance in the gym in search of strength gains. With this in mind, a stratagem is needed that will allow safe training of the fingers and their controlling muscles in the forearms.

Low-Risk Finger Training

Low-risk training of the fingers is possible only if: a conscious effort is made to minimize stressful forces placed on the joints and tendons; a variety of exercises are done so as to eliminate redundancy; a complete warm-up is performed before each session; and plenty of rest is allowed between sessions for complete recovery.

Reduce stress on the fingers by using the open-hand grip for the majority of your training, as opposed to the more natural (and stressful) crimp grip. The open-hand grip minimizes joint strain because it allows a wider angling of the joints while increasing the force potential of the main tendon in each finger. This grip may feel awkward at first, but rest assured that increasing the strength of your open-hand grip in the gym will translate into a stronger crimp grip on the rocks. Avoid extensive training with the crimp grip because of the immense forces it places on the joints.

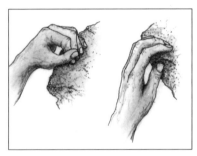

(left) Avoid much stressful training with the Crimp Grip because of the forces it places on the joints.
(right) Perform majority of finger training with the Open-hand Grip.

A wide variety of exercises is key to effective and injury-free training of the fingers. Injury is a sure bet for the over-zealous who frequently rack up long sessions on a single exercise such as the fingerboard. Work several of the exercises described below, never doing more than a couple of sets of each.

A comprehensive warm-up of the fingers and arms is of paramount importance prior to executing any finger exercise. A "cold" muscle, tendon, or ligament can be easily injured, whether training or climbing. Conversely, well warmed-up tissues are much stronger, more flexible, and less inhibited. Start by doing 25 finger flexion/extensions followed by some forearm stretches. Repeat this sequence three times, then massage each hand and forearm for a few minutes – this is excellent for increasing circulation in even the most catatonic hands, like mine.

Flexion/extension exercises will warm up vital tissues and stave off injury.

Rest and recovery time is ultimately as important as training time. A full day off is the minimum requirement between intense finger workouts, and as a general rule the fingers should not be seriously weighted more than four days a week. Although light to moderate finger workouts can be done on consecutive days, such a practice should be the exception rather than the rule. (Note: Some elite climbers train fingers on two consecutive days followed by two days rest). Remember, over-training results in injury, so take two or more rest days at the first sign of tweaks or finger pain. Down time is a valuable investment in your overall fitness and finger strength.

Basic Finger Training

Always start your workout with ATP-CP fueled power-building exercises – those that produce muscle failure in less than 15 seconds. Then move on to the more fatiguing, lactic acid-producing endurance builders. When working the fingers, rest for about one minute between each power exercise and two to three minutes between endurance sets. Rest time is best spent massaging and stretching the fingers and forearms.

Many of the following exercises involve the use of straight-arm hangs. Add these exercises gradually, decreasing the number of sets at the first sign of pain in the elbows or shoulders. Beginners should use loops of bungee cord to reduce resistance; these are also useful for the more advanced climber during warm-ups. Conversely, hang weights from your harness to add resistance as your strength and endurance allow.

The Fingerboard

Many climbers now use the fingerboard as an integral part of their training program. Unfortunately, this has led to a high frequency of injuries. Beginners, and especially persons with prior injuries, should avoid the use of this apparatus. Even well-conditioned climbers should train conservatively and only after a thorough warm up.

Fingerboard training is best performed with the open-hand grip and preventative taping.

Favor the open-hand grip over the cling grip. Other specific ways to reduce your chance of injury: start on the largest holds, and gradually move to the smaller ones; do either straight- or bent-arm hangs – pull-up and lock-off workouts are best done on a bar with the focus on the fingers; use no more than two days a week; and stop at the first sign of pain in the joints or tendons.

A series of 15-second hangs followed by 45-second rests is the best regimen. Employ a pyramid-type progression, using the biggest hold to start the series, progressing to the smallest possible hold by the middle of the workout, then back tracking to finish on the largest hold. A full series should consist of seven steps, with a total hang-time of only 105 seconds. Advanced persons may want to lengthen the pyramid or perform several cycles. Massage and stretch your fingers during the rests.

This might not feel like much of a workout, however there is increasing evidence that apparent strength gains from exercises like this come mostly from improvements in the nervous system, reduced inhibitions, and better technique. Consequently, deep recruitment of muscle fiber is not necessarily a requirement for improved performance.

Webbing Hangs

Attach two small loops of webbing shoulder width apart on a pull-up bar. Start with two fingers of each hand placed *shallowly* into the loops and hang for five to 15 seconds. Work several sets, decreasing to one finger of each hand as you gain strength. This is a good power builder that simulates pockets. Use bungee cords when you begin this exercise, and be careful not to overdo it.

Wide Open-hand Hangs

These are simply open-hand hangs performed on a large bar (2 to 3 inches in diameter) or sloping bucket. Work one minute on and one minute off for three to six sets. It's an excellent pump and very safe!

Forearm Pinch Curls

This is a good exercise I picked up years ago from Hugh Herr – some French climbers perform a similar exercise they call "grasping." Pinch a heavy book or five- or ten-pound free-weight plate between your thumb and fingers. Place your forearm on a bench with your palm up, and do wrist curls, concentrating on pinching as hard as possible. Do one to three sets of 20 to 40 reps.

Reverse Wrist Curls

This exercise, *which is mandatory for all climbers*, will strengthen the typically weak muscles on the back of the forearm that are antagonistic to the strong muscles along the front. They must be trained for balance in order to prevent injuries such as epicondylitis. Perform reverse forearm curls (palms down) while grasping a five- to (at most) fifteen-pound dumbbell or pinching a heavy book. Do two or three sets to failure, once or twice a week.

Squeeze Devices

Squeeze exercisers come in all shapes and sizes, and are made of anything from putty to EVA. Unfortunately, the workout they provide translates poorly to climbing, so their use is questionable except as a warm-up exercise.

Reverse wrist curls. (top) Correct starting position. (bottom) Correct finish position.

Long Traverses

Long boulder/buildering traverses are excellent for improving forearm endurance. Artificial walls with a wide variety of holds are best, although you may have a local bouldering spot that will work well, too. Do as many laps as possible without leaving the wall – try to find frequent rest positions to chalk-up and shake-out. The goal is 30 minutes of traversing without falling off.

Advanced Finger Power Training

Finger strength is generally regarded as the critical parameter for the advanced climber, so safe, effective finger power training must be performed regularly.

The first step in designing an effective finger-training program is to determine your critical weakness. Do you most often fail because you can't hold onto a specific hold like a small edge or pocket because of a lack of power or contact strength? Or do you just pump out on good holds due to a lack of forearm endurance? Many times it's a combination of both, but identifying a "most common failure" will allow you to determine a focus area for your training.

Heavy Finger Rolls

In this article I describe what is possibly the best exercise for developing finger power, which some call "contact strength." No, it's not another fingerboard exercise, instead it's one of the few weight-training exercises a climber will ever want to do. I call it "heavy finger rolls."

Todd Skinner turned me on to this exercise a couple of years ago, and I've since become a true believer. Muscular gains from this exercise are reasonably quick and obvious, and they translate well to climbing. In fact, the dynamic nature of this exercise makes it more sport specific than the long isometric hangs often performed on fingerboards.

Todd credits these finger rolls for some of his most significant gains in contact strength. He first picked up on this exercise from a couple of Soviet climbers he meet on the World Cup circuit in 1987. Todd recalls that they possessed incredible strength yet greatly lacked in technique. To climb well you must have both!

The Soviet climbers claimed that measurable gains in forearm circumference would result from this exercise – a sign the muscle actually grew – while gains from fingerboard training were mostly the result of neurological changes. This statement seems reasonable since the finger rolls cause repeated eccentric and concentric contractions of the forearm muscles. Finger hangs result in no movement and thus are isometric.

Heavy finger rolls should be performed with straight wrists and a slight bend in the knees and elbows.

A long sequence of multiple brief hangs is excellent finger training. Add weight to increase difficulty.

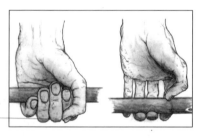

(left) Start at the top of the range of motion with your hand in a closed position.

(right) The bottom of the range of motion is the open-hand position.

Performing these heavy finger rolls is quite simple and requires 20 to 30 minutes. You will need access to a set of free weights and a bench press bar with ball bearing sleeves – maybe the only good reason for a climber to join a health club. A "squat rack" is also useful as a "spotter," a piece of equipment no serious climber would otherwise ever want to use!

As usual, you'll want to do a comprehensive warm up before you perform any serious finger training. Several minutes of finger flexions/-extensions followed by a few 30-second hangs on a pull-up bar and forearm stretches will do fine.

The body position for this exercise is critical to reduce strain on the lower back, elbows, and wrists. Focus on keeping a slight bend at your knees, elbows, and waist. The motion of the finger curl is only the few inches from the open-hand position to the closed-hand position. Ideally you want to lower the bar as far as possible without it falling from your hand. I've found the squat rack quite handy in acting as a "catcher" in case I drop the bar, so it's worth the effort to kick the muscleheads off the rack so you can work the full range of motion.

As far as weight is concerned, it must be HEAVY! If this exercise is to build power you must use an appropriately heavy weight that only allows you three to six very intense reps. After a warm up set with the bar weighted to about 50 percent of your body weight, your goal is six heavy sets with a good rest of three to five minutes between sets. A weight about equal to your bodyweight is a good first guess for a "working weight." If you can do more than six reps, weight must be added; conversely, weight should be removed if you can't do six sets of at least three repetitions. With practice, you should be able to build to 150 percent of body weight.

A few other suggestions: never train the heavy finger rolls more than twice a week. Also, a few turns of 1.5in tape around your wrist is mandatory when your "working weight" is greater than your body weight. Focus on keeping your wrists straight throughout – you are NOT doing wrist curls! Do not entertain the thought of working higher repetitions. Finally, take a week or two off at the first sign of any pain in the finger tendons or wrist because it is probably a sign you're not using proper technique.

SUPER RECRUITING/MAXIMUM POWER

Todd Skinner credits it for developing the outrageous one-finger power needed to climb his Throwin' The Houlihan route (5.14a) at Wild Iris, WY.

Wolfgang Güllich did it for years, which made him one of the strongest climbers in the world and enabled him to climb what may be the world's hardest route, Action Directe (5.14d) at the Frankenjura in Germany.

So, what is "it"? Super recruiting or SR Training! Forearm muscle training with forces greater than what the muscles can lift concentrically. This type of training is very stressful and potentially disastrous; for extremely fit climbers who know their limits well, it's a means to even greater power.

Theory

Super recruiting stimulates the muscle in a way no traditional exercise is capable of. It recruits more motor units than isometric contractions (fingerboard training) or concentric contractions (finger rolls or pinches) and focuses in on the hard-to-activate, high-threshold motor-units so critical for maximal power. Resultant neural adaptations include enhanced motor unit coordination and increased time of activation of high-threshold motor units, which means more power and contact strength on the rock.

The super recruitment is usually achieved via a "falling load," which the muscles cannot lift but are able to catch. This "catch" compensates for very high stress for a brief moment, similar to the plyometric and "forced negative" training used by some professional athletes and body builders. Unfortunately for climbers, super recruiting of the fingers/forearms concentrates greater force on smaller, more delicate structures than any of the exercises performed by these other athletes.

It would seem apparent that the exercises discussed below are inappropriate for most climbers. Unless you've been in the sport for a long time, posses a highly honed technique, and are accustomed to extreme finger training, your time would be better spent performing the safer exercises discussed earlier in this chapter and working on your technique at the crags.

Super Recruiting Training

There are two types of SR training: controlled and dynamic. The latter is the most forceful and dangerous.

Controlled SR

Todd Skinner favors controlled SR performed once or twice a week. One method of performing controlled SR is through a series of brief, extremely heavy-weighted hangs on a fingerboard. Weight is attached to your body (harness) while you perform an explosive two- to four-second hang, followed by a one-to-two minute rest. Your open-hand grip will probably open a bit more as you perform the two- to four-second burst. Be careful you don't slip off the board – if this happens, decrease the weight! Comfortable holds and the open-hand grip are mandatory, as is preventative taping of the tendons at the base of the fingers.

The second exercise for controlled SR is done with a power-grip unit. (For more information, send SASE to Flash Training.) Although this device can be used to perform heavy pinches, it's

(top) Lift/pinch the unit with two hands.
(center) Catching the weight with one hand to super recruit.
(bottom) Catching weight with two fingers is most advanced and highly stressful.

the lowering (falling) of extremely heavy weight that results in super recruiting. The weight is lifted – actually pinched – to the top position with both hands, then allowed to fall back to the bottom position with just one hand catching it. Again, several sets should be performed separated by a minute or two of rest.

Dynamic SR – Campus Training

Dynamic super recruiting was probably the invention of Wolfgang Güllich. In a *Rock & Ice* interview in 1992, Wolfgang described how he trained for Action Directe. Hanging high from a fingerboard or – campus board – he would let go and catch down low, often with the first joint of his fingers. This dynamic-up, dynamic-down training achieves super recruiting of motor units but is, of course, extremely dangerous. You can also do multiple dynamic moves with no legs up a campus board or Death Board, then drop back down one hold at a time. This "campusing" exercise has become a favorite of elite climbers the world over.

One-arm lunging is one form of dynamic super recruiting

Safer, but still dynamic is one-arm traversing or one-arm lunging. Begin on a vertical wall with big holds and traverse a few moves each direction, dynoing from hold to hold using only one hand. Try for controlled, low-stress dynos by using your torso and arms to initiate the dyno and then catching the next hold with a slight bend in your elbow. Shoulder and elbow injuries could result if you consistently catch the dynos with a straight arm, so be careful.

Once you are proficient at one-arm traverses on vertical walls, move on to slightly overhanging sections. This increases the stress on all components of the fingers and arms, so proceed with caution. Perform once a week near the beginning of a workout but only after a good warm-up.

Conclusion

There's no doubt that super recruiting is an excellent power builder for the finger-flexing muscles of the forearms. It is also one of the more dangerous strength-training exercises around.

Obviously, this exercise is best left to advanced climbers, but mature intermediate climbers may want to occasionally test themselves with some light super recruiting. Of the four exercises described above, controlled SR with the power grip and dynamic SR via one-arm traverses are the best to begin with. Always warm up well with stretching and Sports-massage, then tape the base of the middle two fingers on each hand.

Vary your exercises every few weeks, and begin period-ization (see Designing a Strength Training Program) of your training. Super recruiting is best performed during the later part of the preparation phase, then discontinue it as your time on the rock increases.

And remember, more power is good, but better technique is best! Don't get sucked into a lust for power that can get you injured or blind you from seeing and working on the other areas you lack. A holistic approach always produces the best results.

TRAINING AT THE CRAGS

Todd Skinner

Rate of improvement in rock climbing is based almost entirely on your willingness to fail. While much of the joy in climbing comes from steady improvement and confidence-building redpoints and flashes, it takes an increasing amount of time and sacrifice to gain each new level of ability.

As you continue to work up the grading scale, your progress will gradually slow. Eventually your improvement will become immeasurably small. At this time you must contemplate the greatest paradox of our sport: failure is crucial to success and must be ruthlessly pursued if you want to improve.

Don Welsh working one of the many 5.13s at the Arsenal, Rifle, Colorado.

Mike McGill photo

Thus, the most efficient way to ensure your continued improvement is to regularly work on routes that are too difficult for your skill level, fail, and then analyze why. Identify the exact reason why you fell off the climb. Was it lack of power, imprecise footwork, poor balance, inability to solve or remember a sequence, mental blocks about falling or the grade you're attempting, or climbing too slowly, etc. Only when you identify the cause can you work on changing your weaknesses into strengths.

Of course, this will require a modification of conventional thinking. Starting today, view failures as a necessary step to greater successes in the future. You accomplish in proportion to what you attempt.

The expansion of your imagination is another result of attempting a route beyond your ability. If you are having problems with 5.10 climbs, I maintain that you will learn or gain more by failing on some 5.11s than climbing all the 5.9s in the U.S.

By using the traditional approach of climbing 5.9s in order to work up to 5.10s, it may take a year or more before you arrive at that level. If you decide to work 5.10s in an attempt to solidify that level, you may do better. Possibly you'll be comfortable on 5.10s in a few months, but by working on some safe 5.11s, you will likely develop the skills and beliefs to flash 5.10s in a matter of weeks!

And this applies on up the scale. Trying a 5.14 makes 5.13 feel relaxed and obvious, and working something futuristic makes a 5.14 seem calm.

Remember, there is no practical reason to get to the top of most crags. Therefore, the real goal is not to stand on the summit but instead to have the ability to free climb there. Each stretch of rock you attempt represents a unique test of your ability. The climbs you fail on educate you to your weaknesses, as well as they become the ideal measure of your future improvement – the rock never changes but your climbing ability does! And, of course, the climbs you succeed on are what make it all worthwhile!

With this in mind, I must point out that not every climb you get on should be a date with desperation. Spend at least half your time on routes at or below your maximum ability. Chalk up a nice list of redpoints and flashes as motivation and confidence builders. But to ensure an increase in the difficulty of those flashes, don't be afraid to also spend hours on routes you have absolutely no business being on!

> ## The Strategem
>
> - **Work on safe routes that are beyond your ability.**
> - **Analyze why you fail.**
> - **Train the weaknesses you identify.**
> - **Remember how to win. Spend at least half your time on routes within your ability. Build a nice list of redpoints and flashes.**

EFFICIENT INDOOR WORKOUTS

Mike Pont

The terms and the practices of climbing "plastic" have finally found their niche within the climbing community. Those who would never have ventured to the cliffs can now experience the physical benefits of climbing in a very controlled, safe environment. Better yet, experienced climbers can often improve their strength, endurance, flexibility, and mental sharpness quicker in a climbing gym than on natural rock.

If you are at all serious about training indoors, you must become aware of its inherent differences from climbing at a crag and how these differences will affect your workout. Only then can you make the necessary adjustments and perform a highly productive indoor workout.

Mike Pont shredding at Nationals, Rockreation, Utah.

Mike McGill photo

Indoor/Outdoor Differences

A day at the crags generally starts with a slow warm-up on easier routes, which might possibly take a few hours. You then move on to more difficult routes, all along resting and gearing up for the next as you walk from climb to climb. Finally you take some "burns" on a project – again resting and relaxing between attempts. During a typical day of rock climbing you take frequent rests between climbs, not to mention the intermittent rests you may receive while ON a climb.

An evening at the climbing gym is way different! The routes are close together, resulting in little rest time between climbs. In addition, the routes are constructed then marked to be continuously challenging from bottom to top. With only 20 or 30 vertical feet, the course setter must eliminate good rests and easy moves so as not to waste space. Finally, the gear-up time is nil, because with ropes already in place, you just tie in and go.

This adds up to a high likelihood of a "flash pump," hastened fatigue and muscle failure, and a quick end to your workout. Ironically, your rapid decline in energy makes you think you had a killer workout when in reality it was less than optimal. And if that weren't bad enough, premature fatigue will give your friends the opportunity to claim you as "belay slave" for the duration of the session!

Efficient indoor workouts require frequent, planned rests. If time allows, give yourself enough time to fully recover between routes – 10 to 15 minutes give about as much recovery as is possible until the next day. Use this time to perform a few stretches, get a drink of water, or take an extra turn belaying. The bottom line is that a quality workout is comprised of quality "climb time" and quality "rest time."

Recommendations For Indoor Training

Warm up slowly and avoid the "flash pump" on the first few climbs. Although many climbers view the "flash pump" as a sign of being warmed up, it actually signals the opposite. Once you are thoroughly warmed up, get on a few harder routes that are near, then slightly beyond, your limit. Always give your best, and be sure to push yourself to absolute failure on the hardest routes.

Soon your workout will reach the stage where you begin falling on moves you should be able to do. This point of diminishing returns means it's time to lower the difficulty level and do some laps on more moderate routes. Punishing yourself on desperate, tweaky moves beyond this point has no benefit, unless you're looking to be featured in an injury case study. Use this time to improve technique, all the while working on smooth, efficient, and precise movements. Practice controlled breathing and renew your focus. This, and good technique, will help push your workout beyond those of the past.

Build the length of your workout gradually. A rapid increase in workout length and intensity can result in over-use injuries. With time, your one-hour sessions will turn into three-hour "pump fests!" You will also notice that as your skills improve, so will your motivation, thus allowing you to commit more time and effort. In the end, you are your only limitation.

THE SECRET OF SPORTSMASSAGE

Are you interested in an immediate 20 percent increase in performance? How about extra protection against injury? Does a less stressful, more successful climbing career appeal to you? If so, sportsmassage is for you!

With sportsmassage (SM), you will be able to climb longer and harder while reducing the high stress levels associated with performing near your limit. Just ask any professional or Olympic athlete. They will tell you that SM is as critical a part of their "success formula" as state-of-the-art training facilities and a focused nutritional program. In fact, many of these athletes claim an immediate 20 percent increase in performance when they begin regular SM.

So how does SM differ from those pleasant post-exercise massages you've experienced all too infrequently? The secret of SM lies in its use before exercise. When done thoroughly, you are guaranteed increased power and endurance, improved coordination, as well as reduced risk of muscle cramps and tissue injuries. What's more, proper SM is more efficient than traditional massage in speeding muscle recovery and in aiding recuperation from some injuries. Best of all, you can perform effective SM on yourself!

Keys to Effective Climbing Gym Workouts

- **Warm up slowly** – avoid the "flash pump" so you can have a long, quality training session.

- **Push your limits** – once you're well warmed, work a few routes at, or slightly beyond, your limit.

- **Take frequent rests** – regular 10- to 15-minute rests will allow you to give your best to each route you attempt.

- **Focus on technique** – as you tire, work more moderate routes placing a renewed focus on technique.

- **Increase length of workout** – gradually increase your total workout "volume." This will build stamina for long days at the crag.

- **Enjoy your workout** – by making your workout fun, you reduce the perceived discomfort level, thus allowing yourself to push harder.

BENEFITS OF SPORTSMASSAGE

- **Increased endurance.** A long-lasting increase in blood flow is the most basic result of sportsmassage. This means more oxygen and less toxic buildup.

- **Increased power.** Sportsmassage can eliminate many of the tiny muscular spasms that are always present in your body. This means less resistance to movement, particularly in the antagonistic muscles, so that you get more work with less effort.

- **Improved coordination.** Relaxed, pliable muscle tissue is an immediate result of SM. When one muscle is tight it usually causes neighboring muscles to tighten. The result: loss of coordination and a costly loss of technique.

- **Fewer injuries.** Warm, relaxed muscles are much less likely to knot up or obtain micro tears.

- **Faster recovery.** A good massage helps work out kinks and lesions, in addition to increasing blood flow to the injured area. A relaxed body recovers faster! Warning: do not perform sportsmassage directly on sore or injured tendons.

- **Prolonged climbing career.** Longevity in our sport requires proper care and maintenance. SM will help prevent and control many injuries that, left unresolved, would mean a premature end to your career.

How It Works

Traditional massage has long been used to increase blood and oxygen transport by rubbing or kneading the muscle at hand (pun intended). Unfortunately, the benefits of this simple "milking" process are quite brief and have little residual effect.

Sportsmassage involves deep fiber-spreading techniques that produce hyperemia, a dilation of the blood vessels, through the full depth of the muscle. This maximizes the blood flow in and out of the muscle, which results in increased endurance. More importantly, hyperemia is maintained long after the procedure has ended thanks to chemical changes in the muscle brought on by the SM.

Other benefits are increased power and coordination which are achieved because SM reduces the number of small and generally unfelt spasms that regularly occur in the muscle. Such spasms are often unaffected by stretching and warm-up exercises; when left unchecked, they rob you of coordination and induce a mechanical resistance to motion resulting in premature fatigue.

Strokes

There are three main strokes you will want to learn in the months ahead, the most useful of which is crossfiber friction.

The friction stroke is most often performed with a braced finger, however some persons prefer to use the thumb. The motion is a simple push in followed by a short push across the muscle fiber. Friction strokes should be brief and rhythmic with a gradual deepening of the stroke.

Good SM should be applied forcefully, but don't let your masochistic side take over. It should rarely be painful, except when breaking up a knot or spasm.

If performing SM on someone else, remember that everybody has a different tolerance to pain. You are pushing too hard if the muscle contracts to resist your stroke or if the person lets out a "psycho-thriller" scream. The goal of SM is to relax the muscle, not tighten it!

Although SM can be used on all muscles, focus most of your effort on the muscles of the upper body. In preparing for a work out, or for climbing, incorporate SM into your regular warm-up routine. Five to ten minutes of SM along with your stretches will more than prepare you for your first strength-training exercise or warm-up route at the crags. For best results, perform an additional brief amount of SM before each climb or exercise. I have found this particularly effective at preventing the infamous "flash pump."

The most important thing is to produce hyperemia in the muscles of the arm: the finger flexors and extensors (the forearm muscles) and the biceps and triceps (muscles of the upper arm). This will help push back the physical barriers, thus providing one more "extra" on your way to peak performance.

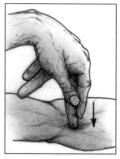

Releasing Stress Overload

Every athlete's body has mechanical weaknesses – areas where movements specific to their sport create stress overload. For climbers the critical areas are typically the forearms, upper arms, and back. They are the first to tire during intense effort and the last to recover. Fortunately, you can slow fatigue and hasten recovery through application of SM to the specific stress points inherent to climbing movements.

Cross-fiber friction stroke performed with a braced finger (top); the direct pressure method (bottom) is static pressure.

The Stress Points

To become familiar with these stress points, it is best to have some understanding of how a muscle works. First, voluntary muscles have two ends, each of which is attached to a bone via a tendon. One end is a fixed attachment called the origin; the other is a movable attachment called the insertion, which is near the elbow in the case of the biceps. The thick muscle belly in between is where the motor nerve enters muscle. It is here that all contractions begin and then spread toward the ends of the muscle as more forceful contractions are needed. Consequently, only a maximum effort will recruit the high-threshold fibers situated near the ends of the muscle.

For this reason we see that a proper (submaximal) warm-up will not work the whole muscle. The end muscle fibers will be missed, which may mean trouble when you contract forcefully during the hardest moves on a route. Thus the ends of the muscle – particularly the end near the origin – are the points most likely to harbor stress and become cramped (see diagram). Fortunately, sportsmassage applied to these points before you climb will warm even the least used fibers allowing maximal efforts with minimal resistance and risk of injury.

Without SM you will experience premature fatigue, along with an increased risk of muscle cramps, soreness, and possibly a muscle injury that might drag on for months. Sound familiar?

Sportsmassage is highly effective on a climber's stress points.

The S and M Session

Begin your SM session with a minute or two of rhythmic compression strokes. Perform these with the heel of your hand. Be sure to work the full length of the muscle. This achieves the initial spreading of the fibers.

Now move onto the crossfiber friction described earlier. Several minutes of this applied through the full length of the muscle will produce hyperemia, which results in improved muscular performance.

Finally, use the direct-pressure stroke on any stubborn cramps or knots. Simply push straight in with a braced finger (boulderer extraordinaire and masseur Tim Toula suggests you save finger strength and use the eraser end of a large children's pencil) and hold for 15 to 60 seconds. Direct pressure is especially useful when applied to the pressure points near the base of the muscles. This will not only relieve any unknown tiny spasms that might increase muscular resistance, but will also help warm up those hard-to-recruit end fibers.

Don't forget that SM should be forceful but not painful! Work all the critical muscles, including the antagonistic muscle groups, until they are warm and loose. This is best achieved through a combination of a traditional warm-up, stretching, and sportsmassage. Do this and your body will be ready for a whole new level of climbing performance!

Sportsmassage Procedures

1) Start with a minute or two of compression strokes, performed with the heel or side of the hand, over the full length of the muscle.
2) Now apply crossfiber friction. Gradually press deeper into the muscle, but not to the point of pain.
3) Finish with direct pressure to any kinks or knots that remain. Hold for 15 to 60 seconds.
4) Supplement the Sportsmassage session with your other warm-up and stretching exercises.

STRETCHING FOR CLIMBING

Tim "TNT" Toula

Before you read any further, put on your loosest sweats, find a warm, padded expanse of floor, and stretch your legs apart. You don't get more flexible by reading an article on stretching. You get more flexible by stretching while you read. So start right now!

Reasons For Not Stretching?

Let me start with a shocker...I know you're expecting me to say that you have to be flexible to become a high-grade climber. Well, you don't! You don't have to be able to do splits to be a conquistador of rad. Flexibility is not everything. In fact, in many climbing conquests flexibility doesn't mean squat. Three of the more amazing climbers I've ever seen – Skinner, Sherman, and Mattson – are stiff as bricks. They could barely touch their toes let alone get splayed 180 degrees. Yet these boys can crank! So take heart. If your pseudonym is Rusty Hinge, don't sweat it. A cranker of rad you may still be.

Reasons For Stretching!

From a rock climbing perspective, the value of stretching is to reach holds heretofore unknown, distribute more weight on the feet, and to keep the legs from impeding progress (i.e. get the legs out of the way). Not until you get flexible will you ever experience unhindered movement, feel the beauty of the full range of muscular motion, and move with the grace of a Baryshnikov. For what is the essence of rock climbing if not movement? And is not ease of movement over stone the quality sought after?

From a more general athletic standpoint, the benefits of stretching are twofold.

- Stretching helps to minimize the internal resistance of any muscle movement. As a climber you're already fighting the external resistance known as gravity. Why fight two resistances when you can alleviate or minimize one?

- Stretching creates an abundance of oxygen in your muscles thereby minimizing lactic acid buildup through more efficient burning of muscle fuels. Like a well-tuned carburetor, your body will get better mileage through stretching.

While we're on it, turn your parents, family, and friends onto stretching as well. Even for non-athletic folk, it will oxygenate and to some degree tone the muscles. Stretching by its nature sends a signal to the body to lighten up. It curbs appetite, so you'll lose weight. Finally, it relaxes the mind, improves focus, and busts stress.

If you're still not convinced, then just trust me: you can improve your flexibility if you stretch regularly. Yes, your ultimate level of flexibility does hinge on your genetic background, but no matter the stock of your parents, you can improve.

Phases of Flexibility Training

The following five-phase procedure is a safe, effective method adapted from *The Book About Stretching* by exercise physiologist, Sven Sölveborn. If you're motivated, it will improve your flexibility.

For any given muscle, perform the stretch in these five phases.

Phase 1: A wake-up stretch. Easy does it! There should be no pain involved, only light tension on the muscles.

Phase 2: Building stretch. More light tension in the muscles but begin to "try" the muscle a bit.

Phase 3: Work stretch. Hold steady muscular tension for at least three to five breathing cycles. Learn to stretch in relation to the number of breaths, not to time.

Phase 4: Gain stretch. Really begin to work the stretch now. Again, hold each stretch for three to five breaths.

Phase 5: Another gain stretch. Focus on making an advance, even if small, beyond prior sessions.

Other Keys to Effective Training

You'll probably find certain joints (or one side) are more flexible than others. Resist the tendency to stretch your more flexible side first. Always work the poor side first. You'll be psychologically fresher and try harder to improve the weak side.

Set both daily and long-term goals for your flexibility. While you want the long-term goal to stew in the cauldron of your mind, concentrate harder on reaching the goal du jour for a given session.

And as mentioned earlier, stretch according to your breaths. Learn to breathe diaphragmatically. This will improve your stretching session. Begin each breath from the stomach, then expand into the lungs. For the best possible stretch, concentrate on taking the fullest inhalations and exhalations possible.

Three Lower-body Stretches

Let's look at perhaps the three most important stretching positions for climbing. Work the five phases mentioned earlier for each.

Pliés

This lateral splaying of the legs is most valuable for face and crack climbing because it allows you to get your hips closer to the wall. This places more weight on the feet and less on the arms, thus minimizing finger/arm-power output. Pliés also make for a creative rest stance from which to depump.

The best way to improve this position is with "froggies". Lie flat on your stomach with your knees out to the side and feet on the floor. The further your knees are out to the side, the harder the stretch becomes.

High steps

These involve lifting your legs high while you're against the wall gripping hand holds. I first saw the benefit and mastery of this skill when in the pre-dawn era of sport climbing, the ol' bouldering maestro, Dick "Mr. Supple" Cilley, would slide his foot onto an edge by his earlobe, which squeaked him through yet another desperate B2 move.

These can be performed on a kitchen counter or on a climbing wall. Stand against the counter or chest flat against the wall. With one foot flat on the floor, attempt to lift the other

Tim Toula demonstrates his brand of high step stretching.

Froggies will help improve your plié position when climbing.

leg up to the top of the counter or onto a hold on the wall. If necessary, use a partner to help push out the last inch of the stretch. They should also prevent you from cheating your butt away from the wall.

Climbing champion, Robyn Erbesfield, remarked to me how this stretch, combined with multiple repetitions for each leg, really made her much stronger at high steps. Flexibility alone doesn't make you a great high stepper, you must also have the strength to get your leg up to the hold. This stretch is the means to that end.

Splits (Front & Side)

In areas like Devil's Tower, where stemming climbs are a dime a dozen, proficiency in the splits optimizes all stemming endeavors. Even on regular face climbs, an extra range of motion will allow you to reach higher, find more comfortable body positions, and forge rests where the stiff-bodied cannot tread. Finally, splits add to your arsenal on overhangs and roof cracks where a far-reaching foot can act as a third hand.

Splits – usually done on the floor, not the ceiling – are another great stretch.

Wall split

Straddle Split

Butterfly

Sitting Butterfly

Knee to Chest

Awareness

Avoid overstretching and be aware! There is a fine line between stretching gains and pain or injury. Here are a few signs you've over-stretched.

- You wake up the next morning and your muscles feel tighter than the skin on a turnip. Fortunately, this kind of tenseness will usually recede in a couple days.
- You hear a distinct "pop" while stretching. In this case, hobble over to the fridge and pull out a semi-frozen "oil can" and put your injury on ice. Toss away the empty, and repeat in an hour or less.
- You experience pain near or in a joint (most likely the knee). You probably stretched the tendons and ligaments in addition to the muscles. Cut back or stop stretching for a time if you experience pain in the joints.

Don't Forget the Rest

While the three lower-body stretches described above are some of the most important for climbing, there are several others you'll want to perform during your warm up and cool down. Listed below are 15 additional lower and upper body stretches that will make your flexibility training comprehensive. Follow the stretching guidelines listed earlier.

MORE LOWER BODY STRETCHES
Wall Split

This is an easy stretch that is very effective at stretching the groin. Start with your legs elevated and together, with your butt a few inches away from the wall. Slowly separate your legs – heels resting on the wall – until you feel the stretching begin in your groin. Be sure your lower back remains flat on the floor.

Straddle Split

This one is another good stretch for the groin and hips. Sit with your feet a comfortable distance apart and slowly lean forward. Bend at the hips and keep your back straight—do not lead forward with your head and shoulders! To stretch one leg at a time, turn to face one foot and bend forward from the hips.

Butterfly

Lie on your back, with your knees bent and soles of your feet together. Relax and let gravity pull your knees down. Some persons experience a feeling that their hip structure is preventing a complete stretch. Rest assured that in time you will be able to stretch through that "stopping point."

Sitting Butterfly

Similar to the previous stretch, the Sitting Butterfly is performed in a sitting position with some added pressure applied with your elbows. Keeping your back straight, lean forward at the hips and press down on your legs (a few inches above the knee) with your elbows. Perform this stretch with your feet together but at varying distances from your groin.

Knee to Chest

This stretch feels good because it loosens the often tense muscles of the lower back. Pull one knee toward your chest while keeping the other leg straight and flat on the floor. As a variation you can pull your knee across your body toward the opposite shoulder to stretch the outside of the hip, too.

Double Stag

Safer than the infamous hurdler's stretch for working the quadricep muscle. With one knee on the floor, step forward so the forward knee is directly over the foot (the knee should never pass forward of the foot). Now reach back with the hand opposite the rear leg, and pull that foot gently toward your buttocks.

Spinal Twist

Sit with one leg flat on the floor and the other bent and crossed over the flat leg. Place the elbow opposite the bent leg on the outside of the bent leg. Begin to turn at the hips and look over your shoulder. This an excellent stretch for the upper back, lower back, side of hips, and rib cage.

Abdominal "Seal" Stretch

Perform this stretch carefully, particularly if you have lower back problems. Press your shoulders away from the floor as shown. It's important also to contract your buttocks while performing this stretch so as to reduce any stress placed on your lower back.

Calf Stretch

Don't forget this one! It'll increase your extension when pressing off footholds, as well as improve endurance when standing on dime edges. Start on all fours and walk your hands

Double Stag

Lower Back/Spinal Twist

Abdominal Seal

Calf Stretch

Upper Torso

and feet together until the angle formed at the hips is about 90 degrees. Relax one leg, moving it slightly forward, while keeping the rear leg straight. Hold the rear heel to the floor and move your hips forward/backward to regulate the tension of the stretch.

UPPER-BODY STRETCHES

Upper Torso (sitting)

Sit on the floor with your arms just behind your hips, elbows straight, palms flat, and fingers pointing back. Slowly walk your hands away from the hips until you feel tension in your chest, shoulders and biceps – a great stretch for climbers.

Forearm/Wrist

Forearm/Wrist (kneeling)

Start on all fours. Position your hands so the thumbs are out and fingers are toward the knees. Keeping the palms flat, lean back to stretch the front of the forearms.

Forearm/Wrist (standing)

Place the fingers of the straight arm (arm to be stretched) into the palm of the opposite hand. Pull back on the fingers/hand of the straight arm until you feel the stretch begin. Hold for ten seconds. Now flex the hand in the other direction and pull gently to stretch the back of the forearm. This is an important stretch but be careful not to overextend the wrist.

Shoulders/Upper Back

Pull your elbow across your chest toward the opposite shoulder. While still pulling, slowly move the elbow up and down to work the complete stretch.

Forearm/Wrist

Triceps/Lats

With arms overhead and bent at the elbows, grab one elbow and pull it behind your head until you feel a stretch in the triceps and shoulder. Finish by slowly leaning sideways in the direction of the stretch to extend it below the shoulder and into the lat muscles. As with previous stretches remember to work both sides.

Shoulders/Upper Back

Upper Torso (against wall)

Place your hands on a ledge or wall and let your upper body drop. Bend at the hips and keep a slight bend in your knees. Now bend at the knees more and feel the stretch change. You can also change the height of your hands to change the area of the stretch.

Arms and Upper Torso

This is a great stretch to finish with because it reworks many of the muscles you've just isolated on. It will also help relieve any remaining tensions. With your arms overhead, crossed at the wrist and palms together, stretch upward holding for one breathing cycle. Repeat several times moving your hands slightly forward/backward to vary the stretch.

Triceps/Lats

Upper Torso

Arms/Upper Torso

Training
Technique

CHAPTER 3

The biggest room in the world is the room for improvement.
Angelo Siciliano (Charles Atlas)

This chapter goes hand-in-hand with Chapter 1, Motor Learning and Performance. While Chapter 1 provides an overview of the process of learning and perfecting climbing skill, this chapter will focus on a few specific techniques and tactics.

The first two pieces titled *The Left/Right Rule* and *Getting A Grip* are fundamental to climbing skill. They are techniques we all employ to some degree whether we realize it or not. The key is to know the effects of these skills and when they should be used. The article on traverse training will instruct you on honing your skills on the rock and developing more strength at the same time!

Undercling right, high step and turn hip left.

Next you will find an excellent description of crack-climbing technique, as written by the original Steve "Nitro" Petro. Although his focus is on parallel-sided cracks, the skills discussed can be applied to almost any crack-climbing situation.

The chapter finishes up with three articles that should be of interest to every climber. *De-Pump With the G-tox* reveals a means to speed recovery from the severe forearm pumps we all know too well. In *Fighting Fear on the Sharp End*, Suzanne Paulson will help you with some lead-climbing tactics including overcoming the fear of falling. And in *Just Tape It*, Glenn Thomas tells you when and why you should tape, along with detailed instructions.

Finally, I should point out that this chapter is by no means a comprehensive look at climbing technique. There is no replacement for one-on-one personal instruction—the best choice, if you have a professionally staffed climbing gym nearby. The second best place to find more fine information on climbing technique is John Long's *Sport Climbing* book, also available from Chockstone Press.

Side pull right, hip turn and outside edge left.

THE LEFT/RIGHT RULE

Reach, stability, and control – three things you can never have too much of while climbing. Although the location and size of the holds and angle of the rock are contributing factors, it's ultimately your use of the holds and ability to spot the best sequence that determines each of the factors named above. The left/right rule is a fundamental climbing technique you can use to maximize reach, stability and control. What's more, on steep rock it can make the "impossible," possible!

(page opposite)

The author on "Soul Train" (5.12b), Industrial Wall in Colorado.

Jonathan Houck photo

Bob Perna styling with a left/right combo on "Blood Sugar Magic" (5.11d/5.12a).

Whether you're cross-country skiing, climbing a ladder, or climbing rock, the pairing of left-hand movements with right-foot movements (and vice versa) maximizes stability. In climbing it also adds inches to your reach, provided you can spot a sequence of holds to use in a left/right configuration.

There are several different hand and foot positions that you will want to become accustomed with. Practice regularly the ones described below. Without these moves you'll never become a technically skilled climber.

Side Pulls/Underclings

The left/right rule is essential for performing side-pull and undercling moves effectively. These handhold positions, when paired with an outside-edged foothold, make for long, stable reaches on vertical rock.

Remember that according to the left/right rule, you must use the outside edge of the foot opposite to the handhold you are beginning to pull on, which allows the hip opposite the pulling hand to turn against the wall. Such a twisting motion may feel awkward at first, but it's essential for placing the most weight possible over the outside edge of the pushing foot. This preserves upper-body strength and maximizes reach.

Back-Step/Drop-Knee

Undercling right, hip turn and backstep left yields long reach.

These foot moves are the legacy of sport/indoor climbing and are undoubtedly the most important positions for difficult moves on steep terrain. When used in the left/right hand/foot combination, these positions allow for seemingly effortless movement through the steep, impossible-looking moves.

The essence of this movement is a hip turn to the wall with a chimney-like positioning of the feet. The hip to the wall should be opposite to the pulling hand, with the inside leg in the back-step position. Again, the twisting movement resulting from the left/right combination pulls the body towards the wall reducing weight on the hands and increasing reach.

Interestingly, the back-step can also improve your purchase on handholds – a definite help when faced with sloping holds on a steep wall! To maximize this effect, drop your inside knee toward the ground (drop-knee) and hip toward the wall, while pressuring your feet in the chimney-like position. This creates a tension throughout your body that changes the pulling force vector of your hands perpendicular to the sloping hold instead of straight toward the ground as usual. This makes marginal holds usable and oftentimes enables you to deadpoint off an otherwise useless hold.

"Rose Move" pull through left, hip turn right.

Perfect Practice, Perfect Schema

As with any new climbing skill, you must proceed through the three stages of motor learning (see Chapter 1) before you will be able to use the move quickly and efficiently. The back-step and drop-knee often feel unnatural and difficult for first-time users, especially those accustomed to more straight-forward vertical climbing movements. Convince yourself that straight-on (neutral) climbing positions are inefficient on overhanging routes, so if you want to excel on the steep routes of the '90s, you must make these new techniques a part of you.

Establish solid schema by practicing the new moves on as many different sequences and holds as possible. Artificial walls are ideal! Vary the orientation and position of the holds as well as the angle of the wall, if possible.

Pull right, drop-knee left into chimney-like position.

At first you may want to exaggerate the body movements involved in doing these moves. This helps code the "feel" of the movement more quickly. However, be sure you always do the move correctly. A common mistake for beginners is turning the wrong hip and/or dropping the wrong knee – because you can also encode the "feel" of bad positioning. Remember, the hip turn, back-step and drop-knee, are almost always performed opposite the pulling hand, as per left/right rule.

Putting Them To Work For You

Before you can put these moves to work on a route, you must be able to recognize where and when they will be effective. Unfortunately, in crux or other high-pressure situations your thinking can get clouded

Right hand hang, left foot push.

by adrenaline, and you may try to force a bad sequence. Interestingly, if you've practiced these moves a lot and developed solid schema, a kind of sixth sense often surfaces to steer you to the correct positions and movements with little or no conscious effort.

But this may not always be the case. If a move begins to feel "barn-doorish" or if you are coming up short on what appears to be an obvious reach, then you may be missing the correct left/right solution. Look for chalk on the side of pockets and edges and on the underside of overlaps, small roofs, and buckets. These are good tip offs to what the proper sequence might be – it likely includes a side pull or undercling in the left/right configuration.

Same goes for steep routes. Except here you will also want to be on the lookout for protruding knobs or pebbles, tiny arêtes or corners, angling edges or buckets, or anything you can use to stick a back-step or drop-knee. Look for rubber marks left by previous back-steppers – this is a key sign, so don't get too focused on all the white holds.

Finally, I should point out that one good side pull and back-step often leads immediately into another. Of course, it would be performed with the other hand pulling and the opposite hip turning, resulting in a full 180-degree change in orientation. With practice, multiple back-step combinations will come naturally and with a minimum of effort. The movement also feels great, which makes it one of the most enjoyable techniques to perform!

GETTING A GRIP

This article explains how grip type and wrist position affect both your contact strength on a hold and your ability to pull down on that hold. Hands provide 50 percent of your contact with the rock, so using them proficiently is critical to climbing performance.

Since the size, shape, and angle of rock holds varies greatly, it's hard to set rules about grip positions. However, there are two basic ways to grip a hold, as well as some general hold types for which one grip might be preferred.

The Crimp Grip

The crimp, also called the cling, grip is most commonly used, especially by beginners. Although it feels natural to use this grip, it is, in fact, the most stressful to the joints and tendons. Orthopedic surgeon Dr. Mark Robinson says, "the crimp grip places high passive (uncontrolled) forces on the first joint of the finger, which in time may result in swelling and even arthritis." He also says this grip sacrifices the full force potential available in the flexor tendon.

Consequently, it would be best to limit your use of this grip to the occasional hold that requires its use (small edges,

Drop-knee as far as possible to lock feet in chimney position (top) and center). Hip turn and drop-knee on a steep wall draws body into the wall placing more weight on feet, making the hand hold more positive (bottom).

flakes, incut holds, etc.). It's also good to minimize your use of the grip when training. A limited amount of crimp training, maybe 25 percent, is suggested since strength does not seem to transfer 100 percent from open-hand to the crimp grip.

The Open-Hand Grip

The open-hand grip, also known as the extended grip, has distinct advantages over the crimp grip. The most important key here is that it's the safest grip due to reduced tendon strain and because the joints receive some support from the rock. What's more, the flexor tendon can be use to its full advantage, thus maximizing your grip strength.

This grip is most effective on rounded or sloping holds, and particularly when pulling on pockets. If you're unfamiliar with the open-hand grip it will feel quite unlikely at first. But rest assured that your strength in the open-hand position will improve quickly if you begin training it. As Dr. Robinson points out, the open-hand grip is so effective that it's also the preferred grip by arboreal apes for locomotion!

Begin training this grip during bouldering or fingerboard sessions. Initially you will have to keep reminding yourself to use it because habit will have you return to the crimp grip at the first inkling of fatigue. Gradually increase the duration you use this grip while training. Soon enough it will become your dominant grip.

In closing, I should mention that although the open-hand position is the favored grip, you should still employ the crimp grip when the hold dictates its use. Clever climbers have also learned to use it as a "change-up" to the open-hand position as their grip begins to tire. Strength (and fatigue) is to some extent position specific, so cycling between the two grips will provide a noticeable boost to your forearm strength on a route.

(top) crimp grip; (bottom) open-hand grip.

The Batwing

Clever climbers also know how to adjust their wrist position to manipulate contact strength with the rock.

First take notice that when well rested, you normally climb with your wrist nearly straight and your forearm roughly perpendicular to level ground. (Occasionally, the shape of the hold results in a slight flexion or extension of your wrist.) However, as your grip begins to tire, it's natural to extend the wrist by pulling your elbow away from the wall into the "batwing" position. As a result you gain a sort of biomechanical advantage that can partially compensate for your loss in grip strength – it's generally easy to spot a tired climber because he will batwing on most holds.

Unfortunately, this batwing effect results in a

Use crimp grips on tiny edges.

Mike McGill photo

Batwing on tiny holds you could not otherwise grip.

biomechanical disadvantage for the big muscles of the back, which makes it much more difficult (or impossible) to pull through a long move or toss a lunge. Consequently, you must become aware of when you batwing, and then determine whether it will be to your advantage or disadvantage.

These are a few situations when it's advantageous to extend your wrist and assume a batwing position.

- When chalking or clipping off a small hold. Here, you can conserve forearm muscle strength by intentionally batwinging. The loss of power in your back is less important because you're not attempting upward motion.
- When pulling down on a marginal hold that you're struggling to grip. No amount of back strength will get you through a move if you can't grip the rock!
- When grabbing an incut hold or small flake. Batwinging is quite useful in these situations thanks to the "prying" action it lends to your grip. This also explains why batwinging is most effective in maximizing your contact strength when using a crimp grip.

As a general rule, you should not batwing, or at least try to minimize it, when attempting upward motion of any kind or when preparing to throw a lunge. The exception, again, is when there's no other way to grip the rock.

TRAVERSE TRAINING

Traversing is one of the best ways you can train for better technique and build strength. Although some people may view it as too limiting an exercise, there are many different "games" you can employ that will allow you to work on specific techniques or weaknesses. In addition, there are many different surfaces on which you can traverse – boulders, buildings, home gyms, rock gyms, and the base of any cliff. At least one of these must be close to you!

Where to Traverse

Most cliffs and bouldering areas have a few established traverse problems on which you can get a long, pumping workout. You can also use a portion of these traverses as a warm-up before roped climbs.

Those of you who get on real rock only a few times a month may want to limit traverse time to one-third of your total climbing time. Use the few opportunities you have to climb at the crags to your best advantage. That means chalking up a lot of vertical distance doing leads, top-ropes, and vertical boulder problems.

Christian Griffith
traversing at Morrison,
Colorado.

Your home gym or local rock gym are good places to get in a good traversing workout. At home, you can perform several mini-sessions over the course of the evening, each one ending with a good pump! A good rock gym may offer a bit more variety in the form of traversing walls at varying angles, although you can add this feature at home as described in Chapter 7. In this case, you can begin on vertical sections to focus on improving footwork, then finish on steeper sections that will help build forearm endurance.

A drawback to traversing on modular holds is that the footholds are easy to spot and feel. This is not generally the case on real rock, and it can result in a major weakness when cranking at the crags. Solutions to this problem would be to have your gym include a traverse wall that incorporates "inset holds," although they are uncommon, or to find a nearby stone building.

Stone buildings have obvious drawbacks when it comes to wanting a complete workout because they are always vertical and the holds lack variety, but they do offer a perfect playground for working on the subtleties of thin face. The best walls are those where the mason tried to make the mortar flush with the blocks. On occasion he probably missed a few spots resulting in a smattering of holds that are generally "first joint" or less in depth. This presents the perfect surface to make you look for, solidly place, and feel your footholds.

The Traverse Workout

With a decent wall and an hour of free time, you can complete an awfully good workout of both technique and strength. Always begin with a good warm-up of stretching and sportsmassage, and then a few pull-ups and hangs. Next, walk along the base of the wall grasping various holds as you would if you were actually climbing. Finish your warm-up with a few large-hold traverses, if available. Preventative taping at the base of the fingers is also a good idea to help protect the tendon pulleys.

The body of your workout, timewise, will be to develop and complete several long traverses that allow you to spend 10 to 30 minutes on the wall at a time. (If you are climbing on a building as suggested, you may at first have to boulder out a route across the wall because the moves aren't as obvious as on modular walls.) To fill this much time, you will need to do several laps on the wall. Better yet, develop a loop that allows you to cross low on the wall using one sequence, then

move up a few feet and cross back on a different set of holds.

Of key importance is the constant focus on footwork. After all, if you want to last a long time on a difficult traverse, or real route for that matter, you better learn to use your feet to every possible advantage.

Below are several things on which to focus when you're traverse training.

- Learn to spot, then feel for, the best placement on each foothold. Many people are sloppy with their feet and miss the best placements.
- Weight each foot to the maximum amount possible. Doing this on small, sloping holds definitely requires a feel that only comes with lots of time on the rock.

Great outdoor traverse training can be found in the busiest city, or the quietest hillside.

- Keep your weight in over your feet as much as possible. Learn to look for holds without hanging your butt way out off the wall.
- Relax your grip to the minimum required amount. This, too, takes experimentation and time, but it will add lots to your endurance.
- Learn to move quickly through thin, tweaky sequences. Get on and off the small, energy consuming holds as fast as possible. Chalking in the middle of a crux sequence is like placing gear in the middle of a crux – you may be successful in hanging out and doing it, but you'll likely have wasted so much energy in the process that you'll fail to finish the crux.
- Learn to get a quick (a few seconds only) shake/chalk just before, and soon after, you move through the crux section of a traverse.

- Learn to spot good rests in advance and work on prolonging any major camping (long rests/shake outs) until you get to them.
- As you tire, renew your focus on footwork and relaxing, repeatedly. Pumping climbers commonly narrow their focus to finding better handholds. Thus their footwork deteriorates and they pump out even faster.
- Don't give up and jump off when the deep pump begins to set in. This is when you build the mental fortitude to push on a bit longer despite increasing physical discomfort – a key to doing harder routes!

Traverse Training "Games"

On a traversing wall you can begin to spice things up a bit by modifying the sequence or changing the way you grip the holds. Experiment with some of the following items.

- Try playing "three-finger" or "two-finger." That is, perform the traverse by gripping

Indoor traverse training

each hold with only the named number of fingers. This will make you rely more on your feet as well as build finger power – two excellent benefits!
- How about open hand. Try to do the full traverse without using the crimp grip. The open-hand grip builds strength, safely.
- Try a "side-pull" only traverse.
- Or "cross through/step through," where you perform the whole traverse as a series of hand cross-throughs and foot step-throughs.
- If you train with a partner you can play "send me." Here, your partner will walk in front of you all the while telling you which hold to use next. Analogous to "stick training" on vertical walls.

PUMPIN' PARALLEL CRACKS

Steve "Nitro" Petro

When it comes to crack climbing, parallel cracks can be the most troublesome and often the most dreaded. Unlike granite cracks where your fingers generally "catch" or "lock" on constrictions, parallel cracks require more thought, effort, and skill because of their smooth often continuous nature. As with anything, you'll get better with practice and improved technique. Unfortunately, most areas possess only one or two cracks that are referred to as parallel. Consequently, if you want to get good at this kind of climbing, you should plan a visit to either the quiet, serene Paradise Forks near Flagstaff, Arizona, which is known for its high concentration of 5.11b to 5.12b parallel-sided cracks, or Indian Creek in southern Utah where there are literally hundreds of parallel

cracks ranging in length from 50 to 500 feet. It's at Indian Creek where parallel-sided cracks are defined because you could run a caliper inside a crack for 70 feet and the size would remain the same!

Foot Technique

Parallel cracks are generally either dihedrals or splitters – long cracks that split a smooth face – so the footwork is pretty straightforward. Dihedrals may require some stemming (one foot smearing on each wall), but liebacking is more common with your feet smearing high in opposition to your hands.

Splitters, on the other hand, usually require straight-on jamming technique. Since your feet will most often be jamming in the crack, you'll be able to let them do much of the work. On occasion you may need to have only one foot jamming while the other smears out on the face, but it's only on the thinnest cracks where both feet will be on the face. In these thin-crack situations, focus on smearing the outside edge of your foot, heel down, on the edge of the crack to provide the greatest amount of pushing power. When you hit a spot with no footholds, pull-up on your jams quickly and try to place your feet on something higher up.

Finally, don't forget to move as quickly as possible. Parallel cracks can have many moves in a row of the same difficulty and no good rests – these cracks are endurance routes!

Hand Technique

Your hands may be used thumbs up or thumbs down and in any combination. With thumbs up you can reach farther, but with thumbs down you can increase the torque of your jam. Use your thumbs inside the crack whenever possible. If it's a tips crack, place your thumb under the first digit of your forefinger for support.

Finger Jamming

Slide or push your fingers into the crack, working them up and down (milking 'em) a few times to secure the best fit. Then twist them to apply torque, so there's pressure of the stone against your aching fingers. Turn your elbow down so your forearm becomes parallel to the crack. Keep your forearm against the rock to prevent your fingers from levering out. If your fingers fit in all the way, then place your thumb into the crack also, as a fifth finger. In dihedrals, almost always one hand is thumb up while the other is thumb down. On splitters, try to vary thumbs up/down on both hands to help prevent cramping of the hands or forearms.

Off-Fingers

Off-fingers or rattley fingers is around a #1.5-Friend-sized crack for most. You have two choices here: go thumbs up and squeeze like the dickens, or thumbs down with your thumb tucked in tight under the forefinger. Apply torque by twisting the hand and rotating the forearm until it's parallel to the crack, thereby removing the rattle. Many climbers complain that this is an insecure jam...Be patient. Exercise some faith.

Thin Hands

Thin hands – approximately #2 Friend-sized – can be the most insecure and also quite strenuous if it's a long section. Again, with thumbs up you must squeeze like the Devil! For me, these jams cramp my hands quickly, and my forearms turn into wet noodles, but with thumbs down, the crack cuts into my skin about one inch past the hand knuckle (where the forefinger attaches) toward the wrist. After 20 or 30 feet, these jams also become a touch painful, so the best solution is to vary thumbs up/down to prevent fatigue and excessive pain.

If the hand jams feel relatively secure, you can use what I call the "frog" technique. Run your feet up the crack as quickly as possible and jam them so high in the crack that you can almost sit on them – your knees should be turned out like a frog. You can then stand up and move your hand jams up until you're straight again. Repeat the process quickly.

Hand Jams

The #2.5- to #3-Friend-sized cracks are the most secure and enjoyable to climb. You can smile and often feel safe about running it out 15 to 30 feet past your protection. This is because you finally have both hands and feet bomber inside the crack. Turn your foot and leg so the sole of your shoe slides in against one side of the crack. Then turn your knee up (or in) so your leg becomes parallel to the crack. Do the same with your other foot. Are your ankles screaming? OK, you got the right idea.

Place your hands up to the wrist, cup the hand, and apply pressure to the side of the crack with fingertips and thumb. When done correctly, King Kong could stand on your shoulders and you'd be solid.

Slightly larger hand cracks (#3.5 Friend) require a more strenuous cup than the standard hand jam discussed above. Fortunately, the crack adheres well to even sloppy foot jams. If you've got big paws, these may not feel too bad, but lesser endowed persons may be able to squeeze in a fist jam.

Fist Jams

Fist cracks run about the size of a #4 Friend for most. Place these jams with the knuckles running perpendicular to the crack, then squeeze your hand closed.

Off Width

These are cracks into which you can jam your whole arm and perform what is called an armbar. This involves levering your arm in the crack by pushing your hand against one side of the crack while the elbow pushes against the other. The outside arm is used to pull on the edge of the crack or on face holds. For your feet, use heel-toe pressure with the foot inside the crack while the other foot smears the edge of the crack. "Levitation" techniques also work well in steep parallel cracks.

Gearing It Up

Camming devices are your best choice for parallel-sided cracks. And you'll need a lot of them for longer classics – up to 20 units for a rope-length pitch and sometimes six or eight of the same size. Rack your units on your harness. For long pitches you will also need to rack some over your shoulder.

I have learned to choose the correct size of pro by using sight and the depth of my fingers/hands in the crack. This takes time and experience and is most difficult to hit for the smaller placements. For finger cracks, I find that off fingers is a #1.5 Friend, standard fingers is a #1 Friend, fingers to the second knuckle is a 3/4 TCU, and to the first knuckle is a 1/2 TCU. The smallest TCU is the ticket when I'm faking it with my fingers barely in to the cuticle!

When climbing cracks in soft sandstone, place gear every six to ten feet and maybe closer with #1 Friends and TCUs. Of course, as the rock quality increases or as the difficulty decreases, you can run it out 15 feet or more. Near the end of a long pitch, place pro no more than chest high, as the rope becomes heavy to pull up for a clip.

Jeff Batzer gearing it up on"White Line Fever" (5.12a), Bellefonte Quarry, Pennsylvania.

Most of the time I tape my fingers and hands to protect the skin. More unique for crack climbing, I sometimes tape my ankles for ligament support and wear long sleeves with tape around the wrists, which prevents the sleeves from sliding up and protects my arms a bit when they're deep in a crack.

For the feet I suggest slippers for tips- to hand-sized cracks. Any crack larger than a #2.5 Friend, go with a shoe built with a midsole.

After all this, if you still desire a parallel-sided crack session, then be prepared for a portion of pain and a full-on upper-body pump. Also, be forewarned that these cracks can feel quite difficult for their grade – on a climb where no move is over 5.10, the entire pitch can easily feel 5.11. But remember that perfect practice makes perfect. Believe me, in time they'll feel great!

DE-PUMP WITH THE G-TOX

Muscular fatigue is a well-known companion of climbers whether training in the gym or cranking at the crags. It's also a common limiting factor in attempting to increase your level of performance while training or climbing. Consequently, it would be wise to do whatever is possible to limit fatigue in the first place and then to speed recovery once you become fatigued. The focus of this article is on the latter idea of speeding recovery.

Speed of recovery is important to climbers in three basic time frames: between days of climbing/training; between climbs/parts of a workout; and while resting on a climb or between training exercises.

Although there are many things you can do – or not do – that will speed your recovery in the first two instances, there is very little you can do to speed recovery while hanging out on a marginal rest on a route.

The common method of attempting to detox (recover from a pump) in this situation is to shake your arm by your side. A few seconds, or better yet a few minutes, of using this technique results in noticeable recovery. Clearly, a lot of skill and experience are involved in knowing just how long you can hangout and detox at a rest without wasting energy and hurting your performance. Unfortunately, if you are climbing near your limit, the length of time you can hang out and detox on a route can be disturbingly brief. If only there were a way to speed recovery while shaking out on a climb.

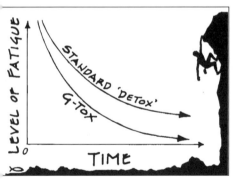

Enter the G-tox – a variation of the standard detox that I've experimented with for the last four years. I named it the "G-tox" because it uses gravity as an ally to speed recovery while at those marginal rests. First I'll tell you how to do it, then explain why it works.

How To G-tox

The G-tox involves simply alternating the position of your resting arm between the "normal" position at your side and above your head in a raised-hand position. Gently shake your arm for five to ten seconds in each position beginning with your hand at your side. If your forearm muscles feel cramped you may open and close your hand a few times; however, focus on relaxing the muscles of the arm as much as possible. Continue alternating shaking positions as long as possible without entering the zone of diminishing returns – wasting more energy trying to rest than you are gaining.

Why It Works

The discomfort and pump that develops in your forearms while climbing is the result of an ever-decreasing amount of oxygen and an increasing amount of lactic acid in the muscle. The blood flow tries to keep up with the task of supplying oxygen and removing waste; contractions of more than 20 percent maximum begin to slow blood flow and hamper its efforts.

While climbing, your contractions are often greater than 20 percent maximum; in fact, they are probably near maximum on the crux moves thus occluding or closing off blood flow. This results in rapid fatigue and a major pump.

When you arrive at a rest, if you use the standard detox method of shaking your arm down, you'll notice a bloating of the forearm blood vessels resulting in the vascular look that bodybuilders pump-up to achieve. The job of these vessels is to return blood toward your heart, but the positioning of your arm at your side, below the heart, makes this task more difficult due to gravity's pull! This explains why the "sickest" pump sets in after you stop climbing and drop your arm to your side.

So why not put gravity to work helping get blood and lactic acid out of the muscle? That's what the G-tox achieves – increased venous return (moving blood flow toward the heart!) Blood flow into the arm isn't significantly affected by gravity, which makes the "raised-hand" position optimal for aiding blood flow and hastening recovery.

Through use of the G-tox you'll recover a bit more quickly than with the standard detox. Better yet, you will reach a specific degree of recovery faster than with the old method.

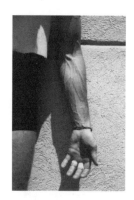

(top) Typical venous flow and the pumped up look of the standard D-Tox, (bottom) G-Tox by adding the "raised-hand" position to your shakeout. This helps prevent pooling of blood in your forearm.

Shaking out at Rifle, Colorado on "In Your Face" (5.12d).

Stephen Dirnhofer photo

Ultimately, it's difficult to say exactly how much the G-tox speeds recovery; however, it is definitely a noticeable amount. Even a modest ten percent increase in the speed of recovery is invaluable when you're climbing near your limit!

One final note: the "raised-arm" position requires minimal contraction of the muscles in the upper arm and shoulder. This fortunately does not affect blood flow into the forearm, but it can become a source of some muscular tension–hence, the sequence of alternating between the two arm positions.

Experiment with and experience the G-tox at the gym (yeah, people will think you are waving at them!) and on the crags.

FIGHTING FEAR ON THE "SHARP END"

Suzanne Paulson

There's no doubt that becoming a full-fledged, on-sight leader is a difficult journey. Deep-seated fears, social expectations, unencouraging climbing partners, a lack of need to prove oneself, and limited childhood experience in falling can hold you back (women in particular). Getting there must be broken down into stages, from leading easy climbs, to working harder redpoints, and eventually to attempting on-sights at or beyond your limit.

There are a lot of good reasons to become a rabid, rope-grabbing leader. For one, when you lead a route, there's no doubt you did the route (no help from the rope). Better yet, the rope isn't wrapped around your face and messing up the scenery. When you look up, there is nothing but rock. With time, your focus will narrow to only the moves at hand – this is when you'll learn your limits and strengths intimately.

And top-roping can develop bad climbing habits such as desperate throwing for holds, instead of using the technique, precision, ingenuity, and efficiency needed to achieve the higher grades.

Learning to Lead

Begin lead climbing at grades well below the difficulty at which you would fall off on top-rope. Learn the feeling of "winning" on lead before you begin to flail on harder routes. I've known people who do themselves in by deciding that "since they can TR 5.12, then leading 5.9 isn't worthwhile." They soon find they are unable to lead at their limit, so they go back to top-roping altogether.

Insist on equal time on lead – even if your partners are better than you. It won't harm them to clean a 5.9 if you just suffered through their fest on a 5.11! The only way to get a good head for leading is to lead a lot, so split time equally with all your partners.

Fear of Falling

If it's been a while since you've taken a fall, or if you've never taken a lead fall, then warm up your psyche by letting go with a bolt or other good protection at your waist. This usually eliminates any irrational fears about the protection failing, or the rope breaking, etc. As for full-on jumping off, I believe it is way scarier to take a premeditated eight-footer than an unexpected 15-footer while concentrating on doing a hard move. Instead, push yourself on hard, safe routes and just let the latter take place.

It also helps to use or discover mental tricks that can help you overcome the fear of falling. For instance, if you are about to try an on-sight that is difficult for you, examine the potential falls before you even rope up. If the falls look clean, then honestly convince yourself of that before you go up so that you can relax and concentrate completely on preparing for and climbing the route.

Redpointing

Another good tool for learning to lead is redpointing. Pick out a "project" and begin working it on top-rope or as a bolt-to-bolt lead. Once you've learned the moves, immediately try

Seth Johnson flyin' at Nationals, Hunter Mountain, New York, 1993.

Mike McGill photo

to link the route into a no-falls, continuous lead (redpoint). This approach is certainly less scary than on-sighting, and it's an incredible learning process. It's also the means by which most of the rock stars do their hardest routes!

Find A Good Belayer

Having confidence in your belayer is essential to becoming a confident leader. I'm most happy when I know the belayer is attentive, doesn't have a sick sense of humor, and has a lot of experience with the type of climbing at hand (sport and trad belaying have different customs). Also, find a belayer who wants you to succeed, encourages you to try things, is quick to warn you if you accidentally back-clip or wrap the rope around your leg, and gets you the rope quickly when you need to clip it. Avoid clipping pro way above your head – the clip is easier and the potential fall shorter if you wait until you're in a stance with the pro near your waist.

Challenge Yourself

If you have a good belayer, the next step is to challenge yourself to attempt harder leads. For example, a few years back on a road trip, my partner insisted that because I "never fall" on 5.11b, I should try harder routes. I protested – 5.11b felt desperate! The truth was that I hadn't really learned how

Lisa Hörst jamming taped hands on "Soler" (5.9), at Devil's Tower, Wyoming.

desperate things had to feel before I would actually fall off. A few weeks later, I on-sighted my first 5.12a and lowered off in a state of shocked elation.

The moral of that story is this: if I hadn't challenged myself on some harder routes, I wouldn't have realized my true limits. This in turn helps me stop worrying when I feel moderately insecure on a sequence. I know how much worse things have to feel before I am truly in jeopardy of falling off.

Undoubtedly, everybody has "good head days" and "bad head days," but overall, leading becomes less and less mentally exhausting the more you do it. The greater the fear of falling is for you, the more you have to be sure to keep challenging yourself on lead to ensure progress.

Attempting On-Sights

On-sight climbing is more adventurous, potentially more stressful, and more rewarding because you're doing the route with no beta, and you have to place the gear or draws yourself. You have no idea whether the route is doable for you. You don't know if the holds are made of cracker crumbs, if the crux is making the third clip, or whatever. Going on-sight may cost you half a number grade, but it does have its up side. For one, you don't have to wait for someone to play "draw monkey" and watch that person flail through the crux. More importantly, people doing the route before you may not find the best sequence and often make it look harder than it is! And that can psych you out.

Decide To Flash

Lead climbing and top-roping are psychologically different sports, so decide that you want to be a successful lead climber, and with time everything will come together. One day you'll attempt an on-sight lead harder than your limit, and you'll have the time of your life. Sure, you'll get so torched you think you can't hang on another second...but you will! Yeah, you'll probably throw a dicey dyno but stick it! You may even "sketch" past the final bolt only to clip the anchors as your hand uncurls from a major bucket!

Surprise yourself – and everyone else – and walk around in a dream for a while. Nothing else comes close!

JUST TAPE IT

Glenn Thomas

Of all the pre-climb rituals we go through at the start of a day at the crags, taping is undoubtedly one of the most important. It is also, unfortunately, one of the least common. Just as stretching your muscles, chalking your hands, and clearing your mind are necessary for peak performance, taping helps out by making finger and hand placements more comfortable and less stressful.

Cracks

Taping first became popular in the 1960s when crack climbers began using it on the back of their hands and fingers for protection against serrated cracks. Although old-style tape jobs limited hand movement a bit, they were worthy sacrifices because of improved comfort when jamming and the reduced threat of a blood bath. Improved taping techniques have been developed that provide excellent protection and freedom of movement. They are also reusable.

Thomas jams up "Linear Encounters" (5.10c), New River Gorge West Virginia.

Rick Thompson photo

Face

In the 1980s some face climbers also began using tape. This was not so much for protection against sharp rock but as reinforcement for injured tendon pulleys near the base of the finger. The concept was simple: a narrow strip of tape wrapped firmly around the base of the finger added support to the tendons and hopefully prevented further injury.

The taping techniques for face climbing have also been honed with time. In fact, finger taping should arguably be used by all high-end face climbers to prevent tendon strains in the fingers. What's more, in certain hand positions the "X" method technique discussed below may lend a little extra strength to your grip!

Taping for Face Climbing

The "ring" method is the most common and consists simply of three firm wraps of tape around the base of the finger. Long-fingered persons should use a .75 inch-wide strip of tape while those lucky people with short fingers can use a .5 inch width. This taping method reinforces the frequently injured tendon pulley near the bottom of the finger. You may be able to reduce your chance of incurring this injury by taping the middle and ring fingers, which are most commonly injured, each time you climb.

The "X" method provides tendon support over more of the finger and may add a bit of strength to the open-hand grip. Tear a .75 x 16 in. strip of tape. Begin with two turns around the base of the finger, then cross under and take two turns around the middle of the finger. Cross back under the finger and finish with another turn around the base. Experiment to tape just the right amount of bend into the finger.

Hand Taping for Cracks

The best tape to use is 1.5 inch wide quality athletic or medical tape, which contains zinc oxide. If you can only find quality tape in two or three inch widths, remember that you can always rip the tape in half as it comes off the roll. With this in mind, here are the three easy steps to a killer tape "glove!"

(1) Rip four or five, 4-inch-long strips of tape that will be used to provide covering and padding for the back of your hand. Make a fist and place these strips across the bony back part of that hand. Be sure to overlap the strips of tape so the entire area from your wrist to your knuckles is covered.

(top) The "ring" method is most common, but the "X" method (bottom) provides extra support for tendons and helps protect skin.

HAND TAPING TIPS

1. Flex your wrist up and down as you apply the tape. This will prevent the tape from getting too tight and blocking precious blood flow.

2. Shave the hair from the back of your hand and wrist to reduce the pain involved in removing the tape.

3. Remove the tape job at the end of the day with a single cut on the front for your wrist, then slip the "glove" off your index and pinky fingers. This will allow you to reuse this tape job.

4. When reusing the gloves, you may need to beef up thin spots on the back of the hand, then re-secure them with two turns of tape around your wrist.

5. Finally, don't be afraid to do some experimentation and customize your taping job to suit specific needs such as extra tape for an extra sharp crack, etc.. Just remember that you are not a boxer, so the only requirements of a functional tape job are free palms and unblocked circulation

(2) Start a strip off the roll that will cross over the back of your hand and comes around your index finger. This strip starts on the pinky finger side of the hand, passes over to in between your index finger and thumb, and then exits between your index finger and second finger. Continue back across your hand and finish with two wraps around the wrist.

(3) Begin another strip from the roll which will cross over the back of your hand in the opposite direction of the previous strip. This strip starts on the thumb side of your hand, comes across the back of the hand to the outside of your pinky finger, and exits between your pinky and ring finger. As before, this single strip ends by crossing back over your hand, then around your wrist for one or two turns.

Repeat this procedure on your other hand, and it's time to go jammin'!

1.) Strips on back of hand.

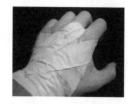

2.) Strip going around index finger.

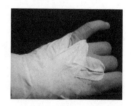

3.) Strip going around pinky finger.

4.) Finished glove with free palm!

Glenn Thomas photos

Mental Training

CHAPTER 4

We lift ourselves by our thought, we climb upon our vision of ourselves.

Orison Swett Marden

Your mind is the biggest weapon you have in your quest for peak performance. It controls everything you do. At top levels, a properly programmed mind is tantamount to success, a poorly programmed one, to failure.

The muscles of your body need training to increase strength. The same is true for your "mental muscle." However, the benefits of mental training are less tangible than, say, weight training. Consequently, it often requires more discipline to maintain a regular schedule of mental workouts.

Over the last eight years, I've read thousands of pages on the subject of Sports Psychology in a search for mental training techniques that can be applied to climbing. During that time, I've written several articles on the subject for *Climbing* and *Rock & Ice* from which I've received a tremendous amount of positive feedback. In addition, I've worked with hundreds of climbers in their pursuit of increased mental control.

The following articles touch on what I've found to be the six most important areas for a climber to work on: staying motivated, remaining relaxed, learning visualization, narrowing focus, controlling emotions, and creating an ideal performance state. I wholeheartedly believe that this information can change your climbing career! I encourage you to re-read it often and to learn to flex your mental muscles.

GET MOTIVATED!

Motivation is an integral part of the success formula in any sport and is a common topic in many sports periodicals. Interestingly, most of the articles I've seen on the subject get it all wrong!

So what is motivation? How can you increase your motivation when it begins to wane? This powerful information is outlined below, but let's start off with what many people confuse with motivation.

Some Get It Wrong

Most articles on motivation focus on getting you psyched for training or competition. They may instruct you to surround yourself with aggressive people, play loud music,

(page opposite)

Lisa Hörst on "Melodie Gaël", Buoux, France.

Mike McGill photo.

find new training facilities, read inspirational stories, look at dreamy photos, maybe even quaff some coffee.

But these things do NOT motivate! They are simply external stimuli that change your state. They may provide a quick fix to your low-energy level for a single workout, but they do not provide the consistent drive necessary for long-term dedication to training and climbing. Once you remove the stimuli, the intensity and enthusiasm quickly disappear.

All In Your Head

Unlike state changes brought about by external stimuli, motivation is a function of internal stimuli. Your level of motivation is a direct result of your thoughts

Expectations and incentives drive persistent, intense workouts. Desire to achieve gets you out to try your "impossible" project at the crags. Unstoppable self-confidence lifts you when external things are getting you down. Your mental visions shape your future realities.

Bobbi Bensman tears it up at Nationals.

Getting Motivated

Below I touch on a few of the larger contributors to motivation. Although described separately, they are inter-related. Review your day-to-day thought processes to determine your use, or non-use, of them in motivating yourself. Make notes of changes you should institute immediately!

Expectancy

Expect success whether you're climbing or training. The best on-sight climbers believe they're going to on-sight the route, and that expectation alone increases their chance of success!

In the gym, both your expectation of how the exercise will change you physiologically and how that change will help you reach your goals, will generate higher motivation. Simply put, you must believe there is a causal connection between your actions and the desired outcome. If you don't, you'll probably blow off the workout, not put your best effort into it, or grab a pizza and beer with your friends instead.

For example, you are more likely to do traverse training if you believe it will improve your technique and strength. What's more, you are more likely to want to improve your technique and strength if you believe it will improve your overall performance at the crags.

For this reason I believe every serious climber should want to learn as much as possible about human performance. The greater your knowledge about training principles, avoiding injury, motor learning, mental control, diet and nutrition, etc., the more likely you are to act accordingly! This is critical to motivation – so read *Flash Training* regularly and leave it by the TV for your slug friends to pick up between B & B episodes!

Incentive

Motivation increases with greater incentive value. In the context of climbing competitions, you may be motivated by the possibility of placing in the cash, although this is probably a greater source of motivation for golfers!

For most climbers, the true incentives are the feelings experienced in cranking a hard climb, winning a comp, or as Jerry Moffatt says, "just burning someone off."

Incentive motivation gets stronger the closer you are to the event or your goal. Set lots of short-term goals, in addition to a couple long-term aims, to shoot for (and hopefully achieve) on a regular basis. Too long a delay between your actions and their payoff makes it more difficult to stay motivated.

This explains why an active "tick-list" (a detailed list of to-do routes) is such a great motivator. If you are regularly sending routes on that list, it'll be awfully easy to train between climbing trips. Oppositely, if your only goal is something broad or singular, such as to travel to Smith Rock or to climb a 5.11, your motivation will be consistently lower. And you'll probably get spanked once you get to Smith or head up that 5.11!

Positiveness

Confident, positive climbers are highly-motivated, successful climbers. Conversely, if you have a lack of confidence or are constantly negative about things, then your motivation is probably about 20,000 leagues under the sea.

Maybe more than any other trait, your degree of general positiveness is something that you learned as a child. Fortunately, a day-to-day effort to turn your negative thoughts around can have dramatic effects on your confidence and degree of motivation.

You must first become aware of your negative thoughts. Statements questioning the value of training or predictions of poor performances may be the most common negatives among climbers. Learn to immediately counter these thoughts with something positive. Use self-talk and self-instruction such as "this will help me build strength," "stick it," or "I can do it."

Rewards

To stick to a serious training program or diet, you're going to need some regular payoffs – maybe in the form of harder leads when at the crag. There are times, however, when you'll need other kinds of rewards.

Becoming a great climber means lots of sacrifice. Regular training, dieting, and climbing often result in missing out in other areas. But an occasional reward for a job well done may be just what you need to stay motivated.

The best application of this rule is to allow yourself a day off from training, dieting, or whatever after achieving one of your short-term goals. Research seems to indicate that irregularly spaced rewards (like those received after reaching a goal) are more effective than regularly spaced rewards (such as those enjoyed weekly). Don't forget, too many rewards in the form of food, drink, or blowing off workouts will sabotage your performance. So resist the peer pressure to participate in the decadence, except on rare, well-deserved days.

Visualizing Success

The most powerful tool for increasing motivation may be visualization. Studies of peak performers in both business and sports have shown they share the common trait of being able to visualize the end result of their labors long before they come to fruition. For example, athletes with long-term goals like winning an Olympic medal were consistently able to get motivated by visualizing themselves standing on a podium receiving a medal.

To motivate for training and climbing, visualize yourself honed and buffed. Visualize yourself cranking through the routes on your tick-list. Most of all, visualize yourself clipping the anchors or standing on top of the crag!

Visualization is most effective when your pictures are bright, crisp, big, and overly detailed. The more you blow up and exaggerate the picture, the more motivated you'll feel. This may sound strange, but it works!

High levels of motivation are necessary for fueling the consistent, comprehensive training and practice that are so critical for improved climbing performance. As your skill level increases, you'll notice that the gains come more slowly and are less noticeable, so you'll need even greater motivation and devotion to improve.

Clearly, everybody experiences periods when motivation wanes. True peak performers, however, are able to maintain or create high levels of motivation through thick and thin. So practice the preceding motivational techniques and always visualize success!

RELAXATION TRAINING AND CENTERING

Climbing is known to demand an equal mastery over the mind and body. Recently, though, many climbers have over-emphasized physical preparation and omitted training the less tangible mental skills. We've whittled down the cognitive aspects of our sport to simply planning strategies and memorizing sequences, but these will gain us only part of our full potential.

In fact, as improbable as it may seem, many climbers would be likely to gain more in performance from mental training than from their present physical training programs.

The mental aspects of our sport clearly are difficult to separate from the physical, as evidenced by the axiom, "what we do with our body affects our mind, and what we do with our mind will have an effect on our body." The most consistent climbers, such as Lynn Hill and Peter Croft, certainly have a well-developed integration of mental and physical training. Realizing the value of such a combination should put you on the road to improved performance.

The first step is to become aware of things you may be doing or thinking that affect your performance. These thoughts or mental barriers can become self-fulfilling prophecies. Even the slightest negative or self-defeating thought can generate worry, anxiety and muscular tension. The antidote is relaxation.

Relaxation Training

Muscle tension occurs daily in everyone. At home or at work, in the gym, in the car, or on the rock, we all have excessive muscular tensions. We all know what it's like to lose our cool on a climb. However, it need never happen again if you learn to regulate your tensions.

Being able to recognize how even slight muscular tension reveals itself in your everyday life will help. You might be overgripping a pencil or steering wheel, or have tightness in your back, neck, or face. Even a seemingly harmless motion such as tapping a foot or fidgeting your hand signals tension. On the rock, tension shows in the way you over-grip a hold, or needlessly muscle through a move, or through a general lack of fluidity and balance. Your goal is to regulate these tensions when they begin – before they snowball.

You will want to learn two types of relaxation: progressive and differential. Both will help you lower general muscular activity and localized tensions, facilitate recovery when you only have a short time to rest, and increase your apparent strength by reducing over-gripping and muscling.

Edmund Jacobson, a Harvard physiologist, developed the training procedures for progressive relaxation. He found that relaxation could be best learned through alternately tensing and relaxing a muscle, and developing a keen awareness of the difference. Regular use of this procedure (see Progressive Relaxation Sequence) will enable you to discriminate between very small increases and decreases in muscle tension. Soon you will be able to eliminate stress and tension at their first signs.

Mastering progressive relaxation, which means relaxing all muscle groups as completely as you can, will aid you in learning differential relaxation: relaxing all muscles except those needed for the task at hand.

Test yourself in this skill next time you go to the gym. Try to relax all of your muscles except those being trained. If you can do this, you've accomplish differential relaxation, but unfortunately, most people strain their entire bodies while working just one muscle group.

Applying this technique to climbing, your focus must be two-fold: avoid over-contraction, the overgripping of muscles being used, and relax the muscles antagonistic or in opposition to the prime movers.

Tension in antagonists can interfere with even the simplest movements. Notice how climbers who try too hard or get gripped on a route become very rigid and stiff, even while performing the easiest moves. Instead of using their muscles optimally, they end up pitting one muscle against another, resulting in more stress and fatigue. On the other hand, the best climbers move with a grace and fluidity. They are masters of differential relaxation!

Skill in differential relaxation comes with increased sensitivity to various degrees of relaxation and tension – something you will learn quickly through daily use of progressive relaxation. Practice by releasing tensions in unused muscles while performing common everyday activities. Whether you are in your car, at your desk, or even lying down, you can scan your body for tensions. Move on to relaxing unused muscles during weight training or performing aerobic activity.

Relaxation skills allow the serious climber a depth of focus needed to power to higher levels. Scott Franklin at Nationals in Hunter Mountain, New York, 1993.

Mike McGill photo

Finally, on the rock, experiment with different levels of muscle tension while moving and during rests. Try to find the minimum level of contraction necessary to keep yourself on the rock. Practice often, and you'll soon be climbing more smoothly and with less effort!

Progressive Relaxation Sequence

Perform the following procedure at least once a day. At first it'll take about 15 minutes, but with practice you'll be able to reach the state of complete relaxation in less than five minutes. Be sure to flex only the muscle(s) specified in each step. This is a valuable skill you will learn very quickly. Finally, it's a big help if you make a tape of these steps (reading one step per minute), then play it back as you perform the sequence.

1.) Go to a quiet room and sit or lie in a comfortable position.
2.) Close your eyes, take five deep breaths, feel yourself let go.
3.) Tense the muscles in your lower leg (one leg at a time) for five seconds. Become aware of the feeling, then let go and relax the muscles completely. Be aware of the difference between feeling tense and relaxed.
4.) Now perform the same sequence in the muscles of the upper leg. Tense for five seconds, then relax. Compare the difference.
5.) Move to the arms. Start by tensing the muscles below the elbow by making a tight fist for five seconds. Now relax those muscles completely.
6.) Tense only muscles in the upper arm, one at a time, and relax.
7.) Now tense the muscles of the torso for five seconds, then relax. As you get better, try to tense the chest, shoulder, back, and abdominal muscles separately.
8.) Finish by tensing the muscles of the face and neck. Relax them completely noting the feeling of relaxation in each part.
9.) Now concentrate on relaxing all the muscles in your body. Mentally scan from head to toe for any muscles that might still be tense. Maintain this state of total relaxation for at least three minutes.
10.) Open your eyes, stretch and feel refreshed, or begin visualization and imagery work. Maybe just crash out.

Centering

Centering is a simple, effective means of maintaining complete control of your mind and body as you head up on a difficult climb or into competition. When you're centered you feel strong, relaxed, and balanced.

To become centered, deliberately direct your thoughts inward for a moment to mentally check and adjust your breathing and level of muscle tension. By doing this regularly, you can consciously counteract any involuntary changes that may have occurred due to the pressure of the situation, such as hyperventilating or hanging on too tightly. Centering will allow you to be aware and to make critical changes. If you don't center, excessive muscle tension and increased fatigue can interfere with your coordination.

Tracy Deufriend on
"Blues Riff" (5.11c),
Tuolumne Meadows,
California.

Chris Falkenstein photo

Centering is a momentary mental clearing and re-adjustment that places you in your most efficient physical state, as well as in a calm, conscious mental state. Center yourself before every climb to develop a base that will lead to consistency of performance. On a route, center at every good shake-out. With practice, it'll only take a second to release unneeded tensions, clear your thoughts, and attain control.

The best means of centering is called the "instant calming sequence" or "instant centering sequence" (ICS), a simple five-step sequence. The ICS is simple to learn and use, especially if you've learned progressive and differential relaxation. Initially it will take five or ten minutes, but with practice you'll learn to do it in a matter of seconds, or even in a single breath.

Practice the ICS many times each day. Use it while waiting at a stoplight or before making an important phone call. Use it first thing in the morning or as a re-energizer in the middle of the day. The more you use it, the quicker you'll be able to put it to work on the rock. Some skilled users claim that the ICS can become an involuntary response to stress. Imagine the power of having such an automatic, subconscious relaxer.

Once you've learned centering with the ICS, you must then remember to use it – this is often the most difficult part! Ideally, you'd like it to become as automatic as chalking up, however, that takes practice. So until then, ask your belayer to yell "get centered" if you become tense or begin to lose control on a route.

The Instant Centering Sequence (ICS)

Perform the ICS while you're in an upright position, sitting or standing, almost anytime or anywhere, as long as your eyes are open and you're alert. At first, take a few minutes and go through the steps slowly. With practice, you'll eventually be able to do it in a second or two.

1.) Uninterrupted Breathing – Continue your current breathing cycle, concentrating on smooth, deep, and even breaths.
2.) Positive Face – Flash a smile, no matter your mental state. Research shows that a positive face "resets" the nervous system so that it's less reactive to negative stress. You'll feel the difference immediately.
3.) Balanced Posture – Lift your head up, keep shoulders loose, back comfortably straight, and abdomen free of tension. A balanced posture makes you feel light, with a sense of no effort in action. A tense, collapsed posture restricts breathing, reduces blood flow, slows reaction time, and magnifies negative feelings.
4.) Wave of Relaxation – In this step you perform a "tension check." Scan all your muscles in a quick sweep to locate unnecessary tension. Let go of those tensions, making your body calm but with your mind remaining alert.
5.) Mental Control – Be focused, positive, and uninhibited about the task at hand. Then go with it.

**Adapted from Health & Fitness Excellence by Robert Cooper. Houghton Mifflin Co., Boston, MA, 1989.

VISUALIZATION TRAINING

If you've begun to practice the relaxation and centering techniques discussed earlier, then you are ready to begin work on possibly the most powerful exercise for serious athletes: visualization (also referred to as imagery).

Let's start right off with an example. Sit back, close your eyes, and vividly imagine the following scene.

You are attempting to redpoint a route you have worked before without success. You're at the final rest before the crux section. You are relaxed, calm, and confident as you alternately shake out each arm and re-chalk. You gently grip

the starting finger bucket. A cool breeze blows across your body enhancing the light, centered feeling you already possess. With steady breathing, you flash a smile and begin into the crux.

Matched hands pull the finger bucket to your chest. You then high step your right foot onto a micro-edge, hitting it just right – it feels like a ledge. You rock over that glued right foot, spot, then grab a tweaker side-pull with your right hand. Smoothly, you extend off the right foot, reach left and snag a two-finger pocket – it feels positive and deep. You stick a high smear with your left foot, and with relaxed breathing focus on the final lunge. Then with perfect timing you toss the lunge, and easily latch onto the bucket that has been so elusive. In utter bliss, you clip the last bolt thinking how easy it felt this time around.

This example of visualization exemplifies a fundamental and important exercise used regularly by the world's top athletes to enhance performance. Although similar to the mental rehearsals performed by some climbers, visualization goes beyond the simple task of reviewing route sequences. With it you can create a detailed movie in your head – one with touch, sound, color, and all the kinesthetic "feel" of doing the moves – incorporating positive images of "flow" or being "right on." You can even imagine shake-outs and rest where you are performing the differential relaxation and centering skills discussed earlier.

Once programmed in the brain, such movies will improve your mind/body integration, thereby enhancing your performance on the rock.

Why It Works

Research has shown that the brain is not always capable of distinguishing between something that actually happened and something that was vividly imagined. Deja vu is such an experience – you can't recall if the clear mental image which has surfaced is an actual memory or just something you've thought about or dreamed.

With visualization you create the mental movie, which with repetition can be programmed into the mind to be reality! Your movie makes a mental blueprint for future actions, so make it as positive and detailed as you can. And of course avoid any negative and self-defeating images because they can just as easily become reality.

Learning Visualization

There are three types of visualization: external, internal, and kinesthetic. External visualization is the most commonly used of the three and is the easiest to learn; it involves watching yourself climb from an observer's point of view. Internal visualization is a bit harder because you are inside yourself, seeing everything through your own eyes. The third type of mental imagery is not actually seeing anything,

(page opposite)
Daniela "dialing it in" in Yosemite on "Cookie Monster" (5.12a).

Chris Falkenstein photo

but instead feeling it kinesthetically. With practice you will be able to feel yourself doing what you are imagining.

Instead of jumping right in and trying to imagine yourself climbing, I suggest that you start with a familiar scene from everyday life, a simpler one that will allow you to focus on developing your imagining skills.

For example, from an observer's point of view (external visualization) watch yourself get up from the couch in your house, walk over to the refrigerator, open it up, grab a can of soda, close it, and walk back to the couch. Imagine clearly what you are wearing, the way you're walking, and what you're passing on the way to and from the fridge. This may seem difficult at first, but rest assured that with a little practice, mastering this new skill will be more valuable to your climbing performance than being able to do a one-arm pull-up.

Next you can move on to internal visualization. In the refrigerator scene above, imagine every detail as you would see it through your own eyes. As you walk across the room, notice all the surroundings and their spatial placement. When you open the refrigerator, see the design and colors on the front of the Diet (of course) Pepsi can which you're reaching for.

With practice you may be able to go the final step and "feel" yourself walking to the refrigerator, the cool air hitting you when you open the door, and the cold, damp soda can as you pick it up. You may even "feel" your biceps contract as you pull open the door.

Uses Of Visualization

When applied to climbing, these skills are powerful weapons with limitless possibilities. But remember that you must practice these skills regularly for them to work for you.

Preparing for Redpoints

Start by visualizing yourself on a climb you have been on before – maybe a redpoint project. Imagine all dimensions of the experience, including all the moves – easy and hard – you can remember, the rests, gear placements, color, and texture of the rock. Create graphic images of how you want to feel on the route – relaxed, confident, centered. Be detailed, going as far as imagining the feel and sounds of the area. The more detail you visualize, the more you will affect your performance.

On-Sight Flashing

Visualization is invaluable when applied to a climb you've never been on before. By studying the climb from below, you can create images of yourself performing the moves, placing gear, resting, and of course topping out. Although you might not be able to visualize every move, you can still create a positive blueprint for your performance. This will certainly improve your chances of an on-sight flash, particularly compared to someone who just walks up to a route and climbs.

Winning Competitions

When they are applied to competition climbing, visualization skills might mean the difference between winning or finishing in the middle of the pack. In most competitions, you only get a brief preview of the route before you head to isolation. Even if you can only remember a portion of the climb, you can still take the wall and its surroundings and create a movie of yourself climbing with grace and confidence. You can program out the noise of the crowd and the pressure of the situation even before you have tied into the rope. Better yet, you can eliminate the self-defeating images that might cross your mind before they become self-fulfilling prophecies.

It's possible that such mental training ultimately determines the winners in World Cup sport climbing, where all the competitors possess similar levels of physical and technical prowess.

"Climbing" Injured/Away From the Crags

Another positive benefit of visualization is that you can imagine yourself climbing even though you may be injured or just away from the crags. Vivid images of climbing can cause low-level muscular activity that approximates the move in mind and anchors motor learning schema (see Chapter 1). This strategy is utilized widely by Eastern European athletes – the most consistently superior athletes in the world.

Climbing Tired

Next time you pumpout working a sequence or route, don't quit – climb it a few more times in your mind. While extended thrashing on a route can result in injury, a few extra mental laps will significantly increase your chances next time out.

Conclusion

Visualization is not daydreaming about the great climbs you want to do or the competition you want to win. It is an acquired skill that requires the same effort and discipline as working out in the gym. Review the tables for visualization strategies that will help you master this important skill.

Visualization Strategies

- Practice visualizing with all of your senses. Work on developing your ability to create vivid mental pictures of people, places, and events. The more you practice, the better you will get.

- Imagine your scenes in explicit detail. Remember, the more vivid the image the more powerful the effect.

- Use photographs, Beta sheets, or videotape to improve the accuracy of the mental pictures you have of yourself climbing.

- Repeatedly visualize the project or sequences you're mentally working on. Remember that the physical practice of a sequence, when combined with mental practice, will yield much greater results than physical practice alone.

- Create many strong positive images while eliminating images of failure.

- Create mental "movies" of yourself dealing with various situations or problems that might arise while on a climb.

- Work hard every day to change and reconstruct your negative and self-defeating images to positive and constructive ones.

- Most importantly, establish a regular visualization practice schedule just as you have a regular gym workout schedule. For best results, visualization should be practiced when you are very relaxed and in a quiet place (use the relaxation techniques discussed earlier). Many short sessions of five or ten minutes each week are better than just one or two long sessions.

**Adapted from Mental Toughness Training For Sports, by James E. Loehr, 1986. The Stephen Greene Press, Lexington, MA.

IDEAL PERFORMANCE STATE

Athletes who find themselves on a psychological roller coaster will perform inconsistently. Conversely, consistent performers like Michael Jordan, or in our sport Lynn Hill, are able to create and maintain a highly distinct and specific mental climate. Consistency on the inside leads to consistency on the outside. Excepting the influence of physical factors, your internal climate will most likely determine your overall performance under varying and often stressful conditions.

It is possible to attain a psychological state that can enable you to function at an optimum physical level. This is called your "Ideal Performance State" (IPS). But how do you get there?

In analyzing hundreds of athletes, sport psychologists have identified ten distinct stops on the road to this state of maximum performance:

- Physical relaxation
- Low anxiety
- Optimistic
- Effortless/Automatic
- Confident/In control
- Mental calm
- Energized
- Enjoyment
- Focused
- Alert

Peak performance will occur only when you learn the feel of each component.

Physically Relaxed

Athletes perform best when they are physically loose and experiencing no excess muscular tension. In our sport, even the slightest muscular tension can erode fine motor control and drain energy reserves.

Top performances require your muscles feel warm, loose, and free. Review the Progressive and Differential Relaxation skills discussed earlier in this chapter. With these skills under your belt, you will have made the first and biggest step in developing your IPS.

Mentally Calm

You climb best with a calm mind. A racing, accelerated mental state inhibits concentration and will allow bad habits to resurface.

You must learn to be consistently calm before a climb, then you can work on staying calm during the climb. This goes hand in hand with the first component – that physical stress leads to mental stress and vice-versa. You will again want to use the techniques discussed earlier, especially the Instant Calming Sequence.

Low Anxiety

Research has shown that athletes perform best when they feel no anxiety, however, competitions rarely come without pressure, and pressure results in anxiety. So how do you minimize or eliminate it? Simply by trying not to get rid of it!

To dwell on the nervousness, or consciously try to get rid of it often results in more anxiety and frustration. Instead, focus on trying to increase positive energy. It is always better to work towards a goal then try to avoid one.

Use "self-talk" to achieve this effect. Say positive things out loud to yourself: I'm well prepared; I'll do great; this will be fun; and smile and relax. Never say anything negative: don't be nervous; don't blow it; don't make a mistake. In sports, playing to not make mistakes will often cause more mistakes. Focus on being smart and confident.

Finding the ideal performance state sparks a climber's best days on the rock!

Rick Thompson photo

Energized

We already know that you need to be physically relaxed and mentally calm, but you also need to be properly energized. Being energized is characterized by the feelings of having fun, being in the groove, flowing, and being pumped up.

When cragging, this feeling is best achieved by flashing a couple of warm-up routes. In a competition situation it's a bit harder, particularly when you've been pent up in isolation for ten hours. Here you can use visualization, self-talk, or possibly some good music to achieve an energized feeling. Also, loosening up on the warm-up wall or stretching will help to enhance your mental climate.

Optimistic

This component might seem obvious; however, it's surprising how many of us get pessimistic when under pressure. Even the slightest negative thoughts can completely undermine a performance. You must be supremely positive and optimistic, no matter how unlikely the climb looks or how long you've been in isolation. Self-talk works best here; the more you use it the greater the effect.

Enjoyment

Although having fun is not necessarily something you might associate with serious athletic ability, it is nonetheless a vital ingredient. You are obviously more inclined to focus energy on things that are enjoyable. Performance problems in professional athletes are common when they stop playing for fun, and instead start playing for the money or their egos. If you are having fun and enjoying yourself, you are probably fairly relaxed, calm, and free of anxiety.

Effortless and Automatic

Top athletes report that their best performance, ironically, seemed easy. They describe a state in which they just "let it happen by itself." Some describe a certain "flow" where they suddenly perform almost unconsciously. For example, Lynn Hill, on the crux of Rude Boys (5.13c) at Smith Rock, pulled off a previously unknown lunge-sequence without really thinking about the moves. "It just happened," she says.

The next time you start climbing poorly, instead of trying harder, ease up and try softer. Doing this will enable you to relax and attain that effortlessness you desire.

Focused and Alert

The ability to focus your attention is a key element for activities like climbing that require precisely controlled and synchronized movements. Even the slightest break in concentration can result in a fall.

Becoming focused seems to require a mixture of calmness and high positive energy. Use the Instant Calming Sequence to center yourself, then visualize past great performances for positive energy. Most athletes find that this works better than just trying to concentrate on becoming focused.

Confident and In Control

These ingredients are, again, very obvious but absolutely necessary. Confidence reduces anxiety and programs you for success. Feel confident and you will probably feel in control of the situation at hand.

Every time you climb, you are faced with distractions or situations that will try to steal your control and throw you into panic. You must stay in complete control, especially of your emotions. Use self-talk and the Instant Calming Sequence before and during a climb; this will help to keep your emotions from snowballing.

Creating Your Ideal Performance State

To build your own Ideal Performance State, use the ten components that we've discussed. Once you can identify each one, you will be able to develop a ritual that enables you to systematically establish and then maintain this mental state, under any conditions.

Every good athlete has a ritual he or she performs prior to a competition. This is a simple, yet possibly lengthy, sequence of procedures used to prepare the individual mentally and physically. Such a ritual will help in creating your IPS by deepening concentration, raising intensity, reducing anxiety, and increasing alertness.

In creating a regular pre-climb regimen, try experimenting, always noting the effect on your IPS and subsequent performance. It will also help if you observe the rituals of top climbers and ask them about their pre-climb mental preparation. Don't be afraid to try something new. It's possible that what you think is your IPS is far short of it.

Zoë Kozub, in complete control, flashes the first of two finals routes at Snowbird 1993.

Mike McGill photo

Once you think you've found the proper ritual to produce your IPS, stick with it. Be consistent. Unfortunately, when under pressure you may be disposed to rush through your preparations or skip them altogether. That, of course, is when you need them the most!

FOCUS LIKE A LASER BEAM!

The ability to narrow and maintain focus is one of the most valuable climbing skills. Widely used, but often misunderstood in the context of a climber's lexicon, the word focus means a laser-like concentration of mental energy focused on the most important task at any particular instant. In climbing every movement possesses a different most-important task, and the best performers are those who can direct their focus to the finger or foot placement most critical at the time.

Before you begin a route, it's common to concentrate on preparing your mind, body, and gear for the ascent. As you start to climb, you may shift your concentration to sequences and the goal of getting to the top. This is all great, but it's not focus!

Mike McGill focuses on "Train in Vain" (5.12b), Safe Harbor, Pennsylvania.

Focus is actually a narrowing of your concentration. Much like a zoom lens on a camera, you must zoom in on the single task most critical to your performance at a given moment – toeing down on a small pocket, placing and pulling on a manky finger jam, or shifting your weight to just the right balance point. Think about anything else and this critical task may fail, ejecting you from the climb as if you're spring loaded.

The most difficult part of focusing is learning to zoom in and out quickly from a pinpoint focus to a more wide-angle perspective. For example, a quarterback starts a pass play with a broad focus when in search for an open receiver, but then he must instantaneously zoom in on the open player to fire a bull's-eye. Similarly, in climbing you may have a broad focus when hanging out on a good hold searching for the next sequence. However, you must zoom in tight as you high-step on a dime edge, lock-off on a hold, or float a deadpoint. If you focus on anything else – your gear, your belayer, your pain, or spectators on the ground – you may as well add a ten-pound weight to your back because it will make the move that much harder!

Practicing Focus

The best time to work on your focus is when climbing a route a couple grades below your maximum ability. Whether you're at a gym or crag, on top-rope or lead, attempt to climb a whole route by focusing solely on one aspect of movement.

For instance, try to do a route with your complete focus on just hand placements. Find the best way to grab each hold, use the minimum amount of gripping power necessary to hang on, and feel how your purchase changes as you pull on the hold. Place as little focus as is safely possible on other areas like your feet, balance, belayer, etc. For now, let these areas take care of themselves – let your sixth sense determine where your feet and balance move.

Chances are you'll find this exercise about focus quite difficult. Your thoughts will wander to other tasks or even be directed to distractions on the ground. If this occurs, simply redirect your focus to the predetermined task, in this case handholds. You can think too much but you can never focus too sharply. It's just this process of becoming aware of your lost focus and returning it to the critical task that will make you better!

Of course, you will want to repeat this exercise regularly but with a different focus (feet, weight shifts, etc.) each time. Work on increasing the length of time you can maintain a singular focus. This will help build mental endurance. You will want to modify this exercise eventually by switching your focus quickly and without interruption between the various critical tasks involved in doing a route.

Making It Work For You

Ultimately, the key to making your focus training payoff on hard routes is concentration and flexibility – being able to switch your focus point and intensity like a laser light show! If you've been regularly practicing the exercises above, the exact intensity of focus should surface by itself. As you move up the route, be in tune to the climb and your body, and with time your focus will zoom in and out on the critical points without too much conscious effort. This is part of what elite athletes call "flow."

In conclusion, I must point out that mental training, like physical training, takes time and effort to produce results. Incorporate regular mental training into your weekday regimen, and you'll soon be surprised by its effects on your weekend climbing. When you get on the rock, get focused on what you're doing, disconnect from everything else, and trust your body to do what it has been trained to do. Relax and go for the flow!

EMOTIONAL CONTROL

Your emotions affect every cell and nearly every function in your body. The mind and body are irrevocably dovetailed as proven by the growing field of psychosomatic medicine. What is on your mind can manifest itself in your body and vice versa. Worry can give you pre-climb jitters and pre-climb jitters can make you worry.

If you are to perform at your peak levels, you must have complete command of both your body and thoughts. An ideal performance state for climbing would include a relaxed, yet energized, body and a mind that is positive, confident and set in the present. Unfortunately, this state is far easier to discuss than it is to acquire.

For each of us emotional stresses are unique, but they can all have the same end result – we choke!

What begins as a bit of anxiety or a case of the jitters on the ground can quickly snowball when you introduce the stress of actually climbing. The chain of events that throws emotions and performances out of whack is common. Observe a few climbers next time you are at the crags and see if they fall into a pattern similar to this.

1) The climber leaves the ground and moves cautiously through the initial moves. They look apprehensive, as if they are trying not to make any mistakes.
2) As they enter more difficult moves, their breathing may become shallow or irregular. They may even hold their breath at times.
3) Muscular tension begin to set in resulting in increased mental stress, which leads to more tension. This leads to more anxiety, which leads to an increase in perceived discomfort and more tension, etc.
4) Their coordination is disrupted. Movements become tight and mechanical. Footwork deteriorates and overgripping of handholds begins.
5) They hold back on moves when they should fully commit. They double clutch on lunges, hang out at marginal rests too long, etc.
6) The fight-or-flight syndrome may be triggered, which kicks in some adrenalin. The resultant burst of energy may help them thrash through a few more moves, but this jolt may also push them over the edge emotionally.
7) The death grip sets in and finishes off the muscles.
8) They soon fall and end the attempt with a long list of profanities.

If this sounds familiar, your emotions have thrown off the mind and body integration necessary to perform at your

Lisa Hörst controls her emotions and hangs on to "Rockin Peacock," Safe Harbor, Pennsylvania.

peak. The good news is that you can change this, allowing for a new level of performance and pleasure to be realized! The first step is to determine the root cause of your anxiety and tension.

Pressure – The Main Culprit

Dr. Thomas Tutko, a leader in sports psychology, identified three pressures inherent to sport: intrinsic, social, and personal. It is these pressures that, left unchecked, charge your emotions and ultimately sabotage your performance.

Uncertainty Will Send You Down

Intrinsic pressures are the most basic and relate to the unknown factors of a climb. Concerns about protection, rests, height, temperature, and ability to do the route are but a few things that pressure your emotions.

The best way to deal with intrinsic pressures is to persuade yourself that worrying won't change the protection, holds, weather, etc., and that you are well prepared and ready to meet this challenge. As far as concerns about whether you'll succeed or not, place your focus on the process only and let the outcome take care of itself. Have you ever gotten tight and shaky on the final easy moves of a climb after walking right through the crux section? If so, it's because you changed your focus from the process of climbing to what the outcome might be!

A Fate Worse Than Death

Social pressures are a result of society's intense focus on winning. Society worships winners, and successful athletes have become our modern-day heroes. If you are a well-known climber at the local crag or gym, I'm sure you've felt this pressure. "Surely everyone is watching and expecting me to flash." It's easy to notice the people who succumb to this pressure; they are the ones who verbalize a list of excuses every time they fall.

These neurotic feelings must be eliminated if you are ever going to fully enjoy the sport. Remember, you are only climbing for yourself and not for the pleasure of others. This goes for sponsored climbers, too, who commonly focus on how they are expected to do instead of just enjoying the sport.

Relax and place your focus in the present. Clear your mind of what happened in the past or what might happen in the future. If you don't, you may fall victim to what is called self-sabotage.

I Have Seen the Enemy, and It Is I

This brings us to the personal pressures that revolve around our own expectations. Most severe is the must-win, must-flash attitude that imprisons some climbers with pressure. Such individuals may shine on occasion, but more common for them is a succession of performance errors and verbal (and possibly physical) eruptions that simply feed off each other. This brings to mind John McEnroe who is known for his eruptions on the tennis court. Interestingly he seems to be one of the very few athletes who can occasionally turn negative energy into championship performances.

Although all peak performers have a strong desire to achieve, it's not outcome-based. Instead it is based on the process. If you are infected with the "must win" attitude, then this is the direction in which you must work. Tune in to and enjoy the process of climbing or competing and let the bottom line take care of itself. Purge all thoughts and worries about how others did, or are going to do, because you have absolutely no control over them. Climb for yourself!

Gaining Control

Dealing with these pressures, and subsequent performance errors, is a learned process – you can't change overnight. Years of getting anxious before every climb or getting angry after you fall are tough habits to break.

If you are a novice climber, begin now to work with these pressures while they are still small. The earlier you learn to react in a positive, constructive way, the better.

Begin by reasoning the pressures away as they surface through the arguments discussed above. This will help significantly; however, any leftover tension will have to be dealt with through Progressive Relaxation. Take a few minutes to go through the relaxation procedures before every climb. This should release any pre-existing tension in the muscles as well as much mental anxiety.

Once relaxed, any remaining apprehension can be eliminated by visualizing past successful climbs or some other pleasant experience, or by listening to some good tunes. Practice and experiment to develop a pre-climb ritual that works best for you.

When you do fall off a route, first take a few deep breaths and relax – you're not a worthless individual just because you fell on a climb. What's more, each time you fall, remind yourself that it's part of the learning process, not a failure. Briefly review the situation to determine your error and what you can do differently next time. Then forget about the fall and get psyched that you are a better climber because of it. A tantrum will teach you nothing and only increase the anxiety of the situation.

In the long run, the mental barriers you break are as important and profitable as the physical barriers. Commit yourself to begin training for mental strength as you do for physical prowess. Ultimately, you may possess excellent technical and physical skills, but you'll never perform at your peak without bulging mental muscles!

Diet and Nutrition

CHAPTER 5

We are what we repeatedly do. Excellence, then, is not an act, but a habit.

Aristotle

I first became convinced of the causal connection between diet and performance in the mid '80s when my brother, Kyle, convinced me to follow his lead and give up or restrict my intake of red meat and white sugar. Being a long-time sugarholic and burger eater meant this was a formidable challenge for me, however, after only 30 days on the wagon, I was amazed at my increase in energy, mental focus, and endurance. This enabled me to work and study more effectively and to train and climb harder thanks to my new-found energy levels. (Unfortunately my brother has, as in all things, taken this to the extreme, and since 1991 he has been living in the wilds of Vietnam on a diet of glutinous rice, bean mash, and raw ginseng root and has withered away to a shadow of a shadow of his former self.)

Consequently, I believe that most serious climbers would benefit by paying more attention to what they are, or are not, putting in to their bodies. A few lucky individuals have a high metabolism, which allows them to eat anything, at little or no expense to body composition or energy. They are rare exceptions. The old cliche is basically true: you are what you eat. Or as I like to say, "you eat fat, you wear fat."

Unfortunately, in this sport where strength-to-weight ratio seems to be of paramount importance, some climbers have gone overboard in their search for the optimal diet. Under-eating or lack of nutrients can result in frequent illness, low energy levels, bad attitude, slowed recovery, and increased risk of injury. Clearly, a basic understanding of the principles of nutrition, and the dedication to apply them, could make a big difference in your climbing

Enter Barb Branda Turner, a registered dietitian and nutritionist I've asked to help set us straight on the subject. After all, there is a wealth of conflicting dietary information bombarding us daily. Barb is an avid rock climber and former member of the Canadian Artistic Gymnastic team, so she undoubtedly "walks the talk." Currently a nutrition consultant in northern Vancouver, British Columbia, she was excited to help set the record straight and ended up penning four fine articles.

To finish this chapter, I've written three more pieces on the much-hyped subject of nutritional supplements. For all

(page opposite)

Tiffany Levine looking very fit at Independence Pass, Colorado.

Chris Goplerud photo

too long, the fitness magazine genre has been lying about what nutritional supplements can do for you. The truth is, the vast majority do absolutely nothing. However, there are a handful that have been scientifically proven to be of some benefit to athletes.

THE TRUTH ABOUT PROTEIN

Barbara Branda Turner, RDN

Protein has likely received more attention from the athletic world than any other nutrient. In the past, high quantities of protein were thought to be necessary for muscle building and optimal performance. Now dietary protein is shunned by some athletes in their belief that it is hard to digest and makes them feel "heavy."

WHAT IT DOES FOR YOU

Protein has many functions in the body that include building and repairing of tissue, acting as a major component of the immune system, and working with enzymes, which facilitate every reaction that goes on in the body.

Growing individuals need more protein than adults simply because they are actually laying down large amounts of new tissue. Healthy adults have a fairly extensive protein pool to draw on; that is, the proteins we consume are recycled several times for different functions in the body. For this reason daily protein requirements for adults are fairly small, even if you are training to increase muscle mass. By far the most important factors for increasing muscle mass are appropriate training and adequate carbohydrate intake to fuel the exercise, combined with a diet containing moderate amounts of protein.

BEST PROTEIN SOURCES

High Quality Protein

	Protein	Calories
skim milk	9 grams/cup	90/cup
egg	6 grams	80/each
lean red meat	8 grams/oz	100/oz
fish	8 grams/oz	50/oz
chicken	9 grams/oz	55/oz

Incomplete Proteins

beans	15 grams/cup	260/cup
tofu	7 grams/3oz	70/3oz
bread	3 grams/slice	65/slice
oatmeal	6 grams/cup	160/cup

How Much Protein Do You Need?

You need somewhere within the range of 1.2 to 1.5 grams of protein per kg of body weight per day. For a 64kg (140 pound) individual this translates to 77-96 grams per day. This is higher than the 0.8-1.0 grams per kg recommended for sedentary individuals by the FDA. Recent research has shown a slightly higher need in athletes, not just to increase muscle mass, but also to facilitate recovery from exercise and to compensate for increased muscular losses.

Fortunately, getting 75g of protein is easy. For instance, a daily diet including a cup or two of milk or yogurt, a can of tuna, a small chicken breast, and a few pieces of bread meet this amount. And this does not include the small amounts of protein you get from vegetables and fruits, plus other grain products eaten during the course of the day.

Some supplement companies would like to persuade you that you need large amounts of protein to excel at sports. Unfortunately, there are no supplements that can do that for you! You need to work on an optimal balance of good nutrition, efficient training, and quality rest.

Consuming excessive amounts of protein places undo stress on your liver and kidneys and can result in dehydration and nausea. In addition, excess protein may be broken down and stored as fat.

On the other hand, our bodies need, and are designed to handle, large amounts of carbohydrates because they are the preferred form of energy for both the muscles and the brain. Carbohydrates also have a protein-sparing effect. If you consume adequate carbohydrates to meet your energy needs, muscle protein will not be broken down into carbos for energy. Muscle protein will be used instead for functions that only protein can perform in the body. Climbers should be very careful not to restrict the amount of carbohydrates they consume. Eat plenty of breads, rice, pasta and other whole grain foods, plus fruits and vegetables at each meal or snack.

The body breaking down muscle protein is often a problem in sports such as climbing where athletes try to maintain a minimal body weight. Athletes must take care not to be too restrictive, or they will find their strength quickly plateauing or even declining. No matter how good your training program is, if your body is not getting adequate nutrients, in the right proportions, your performance cannot improve. Consequently, your total daily caloric intake should be comprised of approximately 65 percent carbohydrate, 15 percent protein, and 20 percent fat.

A consistent diet rich in the right foods can help climbers power through when the tank is empty. Mike McGill shows his stuff on "Pump It Up" (5.12c), Sex Wall, Pennsylvania.

Best Protein Sources

Low-fat dairy products such as skim milk and yogurt, plus lean chicken, fish, or lean red meats provide you with the best protein value for your calorie. For example, a 3 oz piece of lean red meat such as tenderloin contains only 180 calories and 25 grams of high-quality, complete protein. A tall glass of skim milk possesses about 10 grams of complete protein and almost zero fat. Egg whites are the most easily digestible source of protein and contain several grams of very high-quality protein per egg, and no fat. If you choose this option, do not drink them raw like the movie character Rocky, instead cook them or buy a 100 percent egg protein powder which can be mixed with milk or juice.

Incomplete proteins are also useful when eaten in combination. This is of particular importance to vegetarian athletes, who, by the way, are more likely to be protein deficient.

Moderation and balance are the keys to optimal nutrition for performance. Feel free to enjoy a small piece of filet mignon, or barbecued salmon – just don't fry it or smother it in hollandaise sauce – and have lots of potatoes or rice with it! Or, try beans in tomato sauce with a poached egg on top! These are great on multi-grain toast. Bon appetite and happy climbing.

Obviously, fat is not a problem for Karine Nissen.

Chris Falkenstein photo

THE FAT FACTS

Barbara Branda Turner, RDN

With all the attention given to avoiding fats, lowering our intake of saturated fat, and staying away from cholesterol, it would be easy to think that we should stay away from fat altogether. If less is good, then none must be even better, right?

It is true that most North Americans eat far too much fat, which contributes to our high incidence of heart disease, cancer, hypertension, and obesity. However, getting too little fat has serious implications as well. Dietary fat is necessary as a source of essential fatty acids, which are involved in critical physiological processes such as the functions of the immune system and hormone production. Also, all of our cell membranes consist largely of phospholipids (fatty acid derivatives) without which we would not be able to make healthy new cells, including muscle cells. A dietary fat deficiency in female athletes has been shown to cause amenorrhea – menstrual cycle irregularities – that may effect the development and maintenance of bone tissue.

How Much Fat Do You Need?

On average the body's minimum requirement is 15 to 25 grams of fat per day. Usually fat intake recommendations are expressed in terms of percent of total calories consumed daily. For athletes, 15 to 25 percent of total calories should come from fat. This allows for optimal ratios of protein (15 percent) and carbohydrate (60 to 70 percent). Individual fat requirements vary with your body size, age, level of activity, and health status.

For sports such as climbing where minimal aerobic training is performed and a low body weight is desirable, the energy requirements are much lower than for endurance sports or those that require a large muscle mass. Climbers probably need in the range of 1800 to 3000 calories per day depending on their body size, length and intensity of training/climbing, and body-weight goals. Therefore, 20 percent fat converts to about 40 grams of fat daily for an 1800-calorie diet and 65 grams for a 3000-calorie intake.

Fats: The Good, The Bad, The Ugly

The four types of fat we consume each day are: saturated, monounsaturated, polyunsaturated, and trans fatty acids. Although all of these contain the same nine calories per gram, they are not all created equal in terms of their role in human nutrition. Consequently, it is not only important to eat the optimal amount of fat but also to have the best ratio of the different types of fatty acids. This is not possible without first knowing which foods contain which fats.

Saturated fats are most common in animal products such as milk and dairy products, meats, and poultry. They are also present in

CONTROL FAT INTAKE

- Eliminate use of saturated fats in cooking and seasoning. Your daily requirement of saturated fats will likely be met through consumption of dairy products and meats. Use vegetable oil for cooking and fruit jams as spreads.

- Eat fish three times per week. Choose from tuna, trout, salmon, or mackerel.

- Use monounsaturated oils (olive or canola) when cooking savory dishes and polyunsaturated oils (safflower or corn) when baking or cooking.

- Use low-fat or non-fat cooking methods as often as possible: barbecue, stirfry, steam, bake or poach your foods instead of frying or cooking with cream- or butter-based sauce.

- Choose tomato sauces instead of pesto or creamy sauces such as alfredo.

- Minimize your intake of products that contain hydrogenated oils. Begin checking ingredient lists especially on foods such as crackers, cookies, baked goods, soups, and sauce mixes, and other processed food. Becel is one margarine that does not contain hydrogenated oils.

- Replace high-fat condiments such as mayonnaise and butter with mustard, soya or teriyaki sauce, worcestershire, or salsa.

significant amounts in some nuts including Brazil and macadamia. Although excessive saturated fat intake does increase serum cholesterol, in particular the LDL or "bad" cholesterol, a certain amount is needed by our bodies to be made into fatty acid containing compounds such as hormones and phospholipids.

Monounsaturated fatty acids are found in vegetables and oils including canola, olive, peanut and avocado. These "monos" are thought to be the most beneficial in protecting against heart disease because of their ability to lower LDL without reducing HDL (the "good" cholesterol).

Polyunsaturated fatty acids are common in fish, especially tuna, mackerel, salmon, and trout, and in corn oil, sunflower, and soybean oils. The omega-3 "polys" found mainly in fish and flaxseed are currently being investigated for their roles in fighting inflammatory diseases such as arthritis and other illnesses which include migraine headaches and heart disease.

Trans fatty acids are found in trace amounts in almost all sources of natural fats; the majority of trans fatty acids in our diet are in hydrogenated oils. During the process of hydrogenation, liquid vegetable oils are converted into solids by being bombarded with hydrogen atoms – as in the making of margarine and shortening. Hydrogenation in effect converts unsaturated fatty acids into saturated fatty acids largely through the formation of "trans bonds." Recent studies have raised concerns about these bonds because they produce similar effects to saturated fats and may even be more likely to cause undesirable increases in LDL. While most well-trained athletes have a very healthy cholesterol profile unless they smoke or have a genetic predisposition, there may be other, as yet unclear reasons to limit intake of hydrogenated fats.

Because of their diverse, yet equally important, functions, consume equal amounts of saturated, monounsaturated and polyunsaturated fatty acids and minimize intake of trans fatty acids. We consume far too much saturated fat and hydrogenated oil, and often not enough of the polyunsaturated and monounsaturated fats.

Examine your diet closely to determine how you can lower the former and possibly the latter.

In a sport such as climbing where strength-to-weight ratio is so important, it's understandable that fat is viewed as the enemy. One pound of fat cannot lift one ounce of weight! However, I hope you now understand that a deficiency of dietary fat will also affect your strength. Through moderation and a bit of planning, achieving an ideal fat intake is easier than you think! In fact, if there is a certain high-fat food you crave, you can still eat it on occasion without killing your climbing performance. Just be sure to balance that meal with low-fat cooking and other low-fat foods.

FAT FINDER
Grams of Fat Per Serving

0-5 GRAMS	6-10 GRAMS	11-20 GRAMS

MILK & MILK PRODUCTS
[1 serving = 1 cup (250ml) or 1.5oz (45g) cheese or equivalent as indicated]

0-5 GRAMS	6-10 GRAMS	11-20 GRAMS
all milk except whole	milkshake	cheese (except those listed)
2% cottage cheese	mozzarella cheese	eggnog
part-skim cheddar/ricotta	whole milk	1/2 cup premium ice cream
low-fat yogurt	1/2 cup ice cream or yogurt	

MEAT, FISH, POULTRY & ALTERNATES
[1 serving = 3oz (90g) cooked meat, fish, poultry (visible fat/skin removed) or 1 cup (250ml) cooked dried peas, beans, or equivalent as indicated]

0-5 GRAMS	6-10 GRAMS	11-20 GRAMS
cooked sliced deli meat	lamb roast or chop	salami
beef top round steak	pork loin - center cut	corned beef, ground beef
lobster, scallops, shrimp	beef rib, sirloin, loin	fried chicken or chicken nuggets
water-packed tuna	chicken/turkey (dark)	chili - regular beef
clams, crabs	roast chicken	1 hot dog
cod, haddock	oil-packed tuna	2 eggs
beans, peas, lentils	fish sticks	4 slices bacon
chicken or turkey breast	veal	3 sausages

BREADS & CEREALS
[1 serving = 1 slice of bread or 1/2 cup (125ml) cooked cereal, pasta, rice or 3/4 cup (175ml) ready-to-eat cereal or equivalent as indicated]

0-5 GRAMS	6-10 GRAMS	11-20 GRAMS
bagels	1 brownie	granola
all types of bread or rolls	2 shortbread cookies	1 croissant
English muffin	2 sugar cookies	1 piece pie (4oz/125g)
cereals (except granola)	2 peanut butter cookies	1 pc. cheese or carrot cake
pasta, rice	1 cake doughnut	1 commercial muffin
1 pancake or small waffle	1 piece iced/coffee cake	1 Danish/doughnut
4 crackers		

FRUITS & VEGETABLES
[1 serving = 1/2 cup (125ml) or equivalent as indicated]

0-5 GRAMS	6-10 GRAMS	11-20 GRAMS
all fruits & vegetables except those listed)	mashed or scalloped potatoes	potato salad
	10 french fries	5 onion rings, hash browns

FATS & OILS
[1 serving = 1 Tbsp (15ml) or equivalent as indicated]

0-5 GRAMS	6-10 GRAMS	11-20 GRAMS
9sour cream	regular salad dressing	mayonnaise
low-calorie salad dressing	1 Tbsp. butter	lard, shortening,oil

Choose at least 50 percent of your foods from the left column and no more than 10 percent from the right (avoid these like the plague!). Adapted from the Beef Information Center handout.

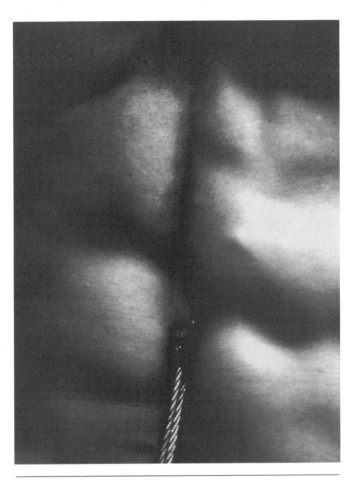

Russ Clune's washboard abdominals say it all!

S. Peter Lewis photo

THE CARBO FORCE

Barbara Branda Turner, RDN

What is the best source of energy for the muscles and brain? Carbohydrates, carbohydrates, and more carbohydrates! Although fat and protein can also provide energy, they are more important for other functions in the body and not as efficient nor effective as sources of energy for exercise. In contrast, the primary role of carbohydrates is to fuel the brain and muscles, and the body can digest carbohydrates quickly and with minimal waste production.

What Are Carbohydrates?

This large group of foods is comprised of sugars (simple carbohydrates) and starches (complex carbohydrates). The simple carbohydrates include fruit, sugar, pop, jam, honey, and molasses and can enter the bloodstream within minutes to provide you a quick source of short-lasting energy – the sugar "rush." Your body soon responds to this rapid rise in blood sugar by releasing insulin to help the cells absorb the sugar from the bloodstream. This results in a rapid drop in blood sugar, a consequent drop in your energy level, and can cause a feeling of fatigue. Because of these results, it is a good idea to avoid simple sugars before exercise.

Complex carbohydrates such as breads, rice, cereals, and pasta take longer to digest and thus provide more gradual release of sugar into the blood. These starchy foods take approximately 20 to 30 minutes to first appear in the blood as glucose. The digestion can continue for up to three hours to provide a slow but constant supply of energy. Make your last meal or snack before exercise one with a good amount of starch and just a bit of protein and simple sugars.

How Much Carbohydrate Do You Need?

Carbohydrates should account for about 65 percent of your total energy (calorie) intake for the day, protein near 15 percent, and fats only 20 percent. This means that two-thirds of your plate should be covered with pasta, rice, potatoes, and vegetables, with the other third comprised of lean, protein-rich foods. Be sure to apply the same rules when snacking. Try to pair up carbos such as bagels or fruit with some protein like skim milk or yogurt. The protein helps slow down the digestion of carbohydrates and results in longer-lasting energy. You can also calculate your approximate need for carbohydrates according to your bodyweight. A minimum for athletes training around two hours per day is five grams per kilogram(2.2pounds) of bodyweight. For example, a 60kg climber would need 300 grams of carbohydrates daily. Since carbohydrates contain four calories per gram, this equals 1200 calories. Of course, a full day of climbing could double or triple your needs, so check the accompanying table to see how you can get that much.

Carbos and Recovery

A high-carbohydrate diet with a bit of protein is critical after exercise to maximize replenishment of muscle glycogen stores and hasten recovery. It can also increase your muscle strength by sparing muscle protein from breakdown during exercise and by facilitating the synthesis of new muscle protein afterward.

In the first 15 minutes to two hours after exhaustive exercise, the muscles are most receptive to glycogen replacement. At this time, simple sugars are your best choice and fluids are better than solids. This is because they are more easily digestible and will enter the bloodstream more quickly.

To complete the replenishment process, eat a balanced meal (as discussed earlier) within two hours. In addition, drink lots of water along with your solid carbohydrates, be-cause glycogen replacement requires three grams of water for each gram of carbohydrate stored. Finally, you must avoid overeating carbohydrates because the excess amounts will be stored as fat!

Russ Clune counts on carbos for steep routes as seen here on "Love Life" (5.12b), Sex Wall, Lancaster, Pennsylvania.

Russ Clune photo collection.

A Word of Caution

Beware of those "high-carbohydrate foods" that are actually high in fat! For instance, most commercial muffins or scones contain three to six tsps. of fat that can amount to 270 calories from fat alone. Also, certain cooking methods can turn great carbohydrate foods into high-fat nightmares. Watch out for pasta with cream or pesto sauce, instant Ramen noodles (which are fried before drying), and of course, all deep-fried foods such as doughnuts and french fries. These all contain more calories from fat than from carbohydrates.

Nuts and seeds are also high in fat and are not a good choice after exercise. One-half cup of dry-roasted mixed nuts contains more than 20 grams of fat and approximately 450 calories. This is great for all-day hikes or big walls but not for a day of cragging, which requires short bursts of maximal energy.

SELECTED HIGH-CARBOHYDRATE FOODS

Food	Carbohydrate (grams)	Calories
Fruits		
Apple	32	125
Banana	27	105
Fruit juice (7 oz most kinds)	27	110
Raisins (3.5 oz)	60	250
Veggies		
Corn (3.5 oz)	19	80
Beans (7 oz)	50	250
Potato (medium size with skin)	50	220
Grains		
Bread (1 slice)	13	75
Bagel	40	200
Muffin (large)	45	300
Pancakes (three 4-inch cakes)	25	200
Cereal (cooked)	25	140
Pasta (4 oz)	100	400
Rice (4 oz)	100	400
Sweets		
Fig Bars (4)	40	200
Chocolate chip (4 small)	28	200

HIGH PERFORMANCE BODY

Your body is like a high-performance car. It needs copious amounts of just the right type of fuel to run properly. If you starve yourself, eat infrequent meals, or consume the wrong fuel, you are likely to "hit the wall." Your muscles rely on carbohydrates to power a lunge, crank a steep crack, pull through a roof, or pump up a heinous crux sequence. So don't run out of gas!

Pack in bagels, bananas, "energy bars," orange juice, sports drinks, and lots of water to the crag. Don't wait until you're lightheaded, weak, losing your concentration, and flailing on a route before you start eating. Small, regular snacks may just be your ticket to the top.

ENERGY LEVELS - THE GLYCEMIC INDEX

Barbara Branda Turner, RDN

Just when you thought you had it all figured out – complex carbohydrates before climbing for lasting energy, simple carbos after exercises for rapid recovery—nature throws a twist in our attempts to simplify and understand the subject. New research in the metabolism of carbohydrates has shown dramatic differences in the energy provided by seemingly similar carbohydrate food stuffs.

Clearly, the ability to control your energy levels is critical to athletic performance. Consequently, you will want to know how different foods affect your energy and moods and this is finally possible through use of the Glycemic Index.

Carbos: Antiquated Classification?

Up to this point, nutritionists have classified carbohydrate containing foods into two groups. The first is simple carbohydrates – sugars commonly contained in candy, fruit juices, jam, honey, etc.

The second group is complex carbohydrates – starchy foods including breads, cereals, all grain products, legumes, potatoes, and other root vegetables.

We have based much of our dietary recommendations on the theory that starches are more slowly absorbed than sugars. The consequent insulin response is smaller allowing for a gradual, moderate rise in blood sugar. This process makes starches the best source of energy prior to your workout because its energy release is slow and long-lasting.

On the other hand, dietary sugars are absorbed quickly resulting in a rapid rise in blood sugar. This elicits a large insulin response to return blood-sugar levels to a more moderate level. Unfortunately, this spike in blood glucose plays havoc with your energy levels, and will often result in a feeling of fatigue or weakness – definitely not what you want before climbing or working out!

Although this concept holds true in general, recent studies are finding that there is a large variability in the rise in blood sugar following the ingestion of various foods from both the sugars and starches groups. In fact, some starchy foods such as potatoes cause a greater rise in blood sugar than certain sugars such as sucrose.

The Glycemic Index

To investigate and more accurately classify the metabolism of carbohydrates, researchers developed the Glycemic Index (GI). This new index determines how the ingestion of a particular food affects blood-sugar levels in comparison to the ingestion of straight glucose.

Foods with a low Glycemic Index cause the smallest change in blood sugar while foods with a high GI result in a sharp spike in blood-sugar levels.

Thus far studies have not been able to determine exactly what causes the different Glycemic Index values. It's difficult to say exactly why some sugars have less of an effect on blood-sugar levels than some starches – a fact that contradicts our old understanding of simple and complex carbohydrates.

Here are a few theories about what determines a food's Glycemic Index and its consequent effect on your energy levels. Use these as guidelines when planning your meals.

COMMON FOODS & THEIR GLYCEMIC INDEX

Peanuts	10
Soya beans	15
Barley	22
Fructose	25
Lentils	29
Beans (dry)	31
Yogurt	32
Milk	34
Ice Cream	35
Apples	39
Beans (canned)	40
Oranges/O.J.	42
Grapes	44
Porridge oats	48
Pasta	45-50
Sucrose	50
Peas (frozen)	53
Mars Bar	60
Bananas	62
Raisins	64
Shredded Wheat	65
White bread	69
Rice	70
Corn Flakes	80
Honey	85
Carrots	92
Potato (baked)	98
Glucose	100

1. Degree of processing – Highly processed foods (e.g. instant foods and those processed under a high temperature or pressure) tend to elicit a higher glycemic response than the same food in a less processed state. For example, instant rolled oats have a higher GI than regular rolled oats, and cooked vegetables have a higher GI than raw.

2. Food form – Powdered or ground foods tend to have a higher GI than their whole counterparts. For example, rice flour has a higher GI than rice in its whole form. Also, foods consumed in a liquid form tend to have a higher GI than foods in a solid form.

3. Fiber content – Soluble fibers such as guar and pectin have been found to reduce the Glycemic Index while insoluble fiber, such as that found in wheat and brown rice, seems to have little effect on the GI.

4. Rate of food ingestion – Slowly ingested foods tend to result in a lower GI than the same foods when rapidly ingested.

5. Starch/protein and starch/fat interactions – The presence of protein or fat appears to reduce the glycemic response of certain carbohydrates.

6. Sodium – Adding salt to a food can increase its glycemic response.
7. Level of stress while eating – Carbohydrate metabolism is affected by your emotional state. Stressful situations slow blood flow to your gastro-intestinal tract hindering digestion and motility. This can result in an erratic glycemic response.

Using the Glycemic Index

To increase your energy and improve your performance, memorize the indexes of foods you eat on a regular basis (or copy the GI Table), and apply this knowledge to determine which food is best eaten before, during, and after climbing or a workout.

Choose foods with a low GI, such as oatmeal, an apple or orange, or yogurt, as a pre-climbing snack. The longer the time before exercising, the lower the GI should be of the food you choose.

After your workout, go for foods with a high GI such as glucose-containing sports drinks, potatoes, bread, or white rice. Such high GI foods will immediately begin to replace muscle glycogen stores – the main source of energy for climbers – thus speeding recovery.

Experiment To Find What Works Best

There is some individual variability in carbohydrate metabolism. For instance, bananas may cause a blood-sugar spike for some individuals while others receive sustained energy from them. Experiment with various foods and listen to your body to determine what works best for you under different conditions. Remember that emotions common to climbing such as excitement, fear, and stress will affect your digestion. You can minimize stress by eating slowly, listening to relaxing music, and sitting still while you eat.

Planning Your Eating For Success

If possible, plan your meals a day at a time. This is important because eating foods with a low GI at one meal can lower the glycemic response to foods eaten at the next. If you're planning an afternoon workout or climb, then include some low GI foods at breakfast as well. This will slow down the use of the carbos you eat at lunch and help provide longer-lasting energy during the afternoon.

Extra Thought, Extra Energy

Using the Glycemic Index to prepare the perfect meal does require a little extra thought, but so does developing the perfect workout or the perfect sequence on a route. So if more power and endurance is what you're looking for, begin paying as much attention to what you do in the kitchen as to what you do while you're at the gym or on the rock!

DO YOU BELIEVE IN MAGIC?

If you have ever opened one of the muscle mags, I'm sure you've read articles and advertisements that have you wanting to believe in magic. Sure the ads are convincing with their liberal use of pseudo-scientific terms like "anabolic igniter," "super lipotropic," and "bio-enzymatic acceleration complex" and their promises of "increasing protein synthesis," "doubling endurance in a few weeks," and "increasing your genetic potential."

It would be nice, but I'm sorry to say that it's all a bunch of gimmickry. Nutritional supplements will not "increase your genetic potential," any more than drinking Coors Light beer will attract bikini-clad women. What's more, any actual gains realized while on these products are the result of the training program the company provides with the supplement and your renewed dedication to eating healthfully.

The Big Claims – Taking A Fall

With all the fraudulent advertising claims connected with many of the supplements and the billions of dollars bilked out of gullible athletes, the Food and Drug Administration (FDA) and Federal Trade Commission (FTC) have just recently begun to crack down. Weider, the supplement mega-giant, was recently mandated by the FTC to eliminate some of their strongest claims and add the following disclaimer to their ads: "As with all supplements, use of these products will not promote faster or greater muscular gains." Unbelievably, the FTC has not yet required other supplement companies to carry the same disclaimer, even though their product claims are just as outrageous as Weider's.

The Hard Facts

1.) No over-the-counter products are anabolic! Some drugs such as certain steroids are anabolic, but they'd be of questionable use for a climber since excess muscle is as bad as excess fat.
2.) Most nutritional supplements are simply food. They add nothing that three square meals won't provide.
3.) There are a few over-the-counter ergogenic (performance enhancing) drugs like caffeine.
4.) There are also a few herbs (ephedra and ginseng) that have been proven in double-blind studies to have some ergogenic effects when taken in a concentrated form.
5.) Recent research has shown there are a few vitamins and minerals such as vitamins E and C and chromium that may be of some value to athletes when taken at greater than RDA amounts.
6.) Supplement powders that contain high quality protein may be of use to athletes who eat very little meat or are on a diet.

Sue McDevitt on "Lunatic
Fringe" (5.10c), at
Reed's Pinnacle,
Yosemite Valley,
California.

Chris Falkenstein photo

The Bottom Line

The quickest means to increase performance on the rock
is through a dedicated effort to improve your technique,
mental control, upper-body strength, and diet. Unless you
are already well honed in these four areas, the few supplements that do work will be of minimal use and may not
have noticeable effects. However, if you have honed your
skills and are both physically and mentally fit, you may be
able to improve your performance through use of the few
proven products.

Weight Loss Programs

A few supplements may have some value when restricting
your diet in an attempt to lose weight. Although crash diets
are a bad idea, you may want to drop some weight safely
without suffering the standard loss of energy and muscle.
Use of a good supplement powder will help ensure you
receive enough protein (1.2 - 1.5 grams per Kg bodyweight
per day) along with the required vitamins.

Beware! Not all the powders or systems you see in your
local health food stores (see table) are created equal. Some

possess mega-calories, many contain low-quality protein, and most are very high priced. Here are a few guidelines to follow if you are in the market for one of these powders.

1) The calories per serving should be low (100 to 300). Even when on a diet you should eat most of your calories, not drink them. Use the powders as a source of protein to complement your meals.

2) The protein should come from one or a combination of the following high-quality sources: albumen (egg protein), casein (milk protein), or lactalbumin (whey protein). The best brands will likely list a PER value (protein efficiency ratio) of 3.5 or higher.

3) Avoid the low- and highest-priced products. The low-priced powders may contain low-grade protein. The high-priced ones are generally the result of the high-cost print ads with "steroid-filled" bodybuilder endorsements.

POPULAR SUPPLEMENT POWDERS & "SYSTEMS"

COMPANY & PRODUCT	NUTRIENTS	SERVINGS	COST	GRADE
Champion -				
Metabolol II	p/c/v	15	$28.99	C
Challenge -				
95% Soy Protein	p	16	$9.49	C-
Cybergenics - *TBS*	p/v	60 days	$139.99	F
ICOPRO - *ICP*	p/c/v	60 days	$99.99	F
Myosystems - *MET-RX*	p/c/v	20	$60.00	B+
Nature's Best -				
Perfect 1100	p/c/v	20	$36.99	D
Next Nutrition -				
Designer Whey Protein	p	41	$39.95	A
Strength System -				
Right Stuff	p/c/v	15	$39.99	D-
AST Research -				
VYOPRO Whey Protein	p	32	$34.95	A
Twin Labs -				
Gain Fuel 1000	p/c/v	10	$29.99	D
VitaLife -				
100% Egg Protein	p	32	$28.95	B
Weider - *Dynamic*				
Muscle Builder	p/c/v	38	$24.99	C-
EAS - *MYOPLEX Plus*				
(meal replacement)	p/c/v	20	$54.95	A-

Note: Grade is based on usefulness and quality of the product, value relative to cost, and ethics in advertising. Nutrients contained in significant amounts: p=protein, c=carbohydrates, v=vitamins. Cost is the manufacturer's suggested retail.

SPORTS DRINKS

Each summer we are blitzed with sports drink advertisements claiming a wide variety of performance-enhancing effects. One drink claims to "help you go faster, harder, and longer" while another says it's been "proven to slow lactic acid build-up during intense exercise thus decreasing fatigue."

Unbelievable as it may seem, there may actually be some truth to these claims! Unlike the majority of sports supplements on the market whose claims are mainly bogus, sports drinks do have some ergogenic effects. But be forewarned, not all sports drinks are created equal! Let's take a brief look into the composition and best use of these special potions.

The Ingredients

The "active ingredients" in these products fall into two main categories: electrolytes and fuel replacements. A simple understanding of both will help you understand how they work.

Electrolytes

Electrolytes such as potassium, magnesium, calcium, sodium and chloride are critical for concentration, energy production, nerve transmission, and muscle contraction. Fortunately, electrolyte loss during exercise is quite slow, so even a full day of climbing won't cause significant depletion. A reasonable breakfast and dinner each day should provide you with all the electrolytes you need. However, if you're heading into the mountains or up a big wall you may need some supplementation.

Fuel Sources

The fuel sources in the sports drinks are mainly carbohydrates, including glucose, sucrose, fructose, maltodextrin (a polymer of glucose molecules) and lactates. Glucose and sucrose (table sugar) are the fuel sources in the original sports drink Gatorade and have since been adopted by many other companies. Ironically, many serious athletes now shun drinks with large amounts of glucose and sucrose to avoid a blood-sugar "spike," which provides a quick increase, then crash in blood glucose, that may actually decrease performance!

It would be wise to pick a drink containing either fructose or glucose polymers (like maltodextrin) because they provide a more sustained release of energy and prevent the "sugar rush/crash."

Cytomax

New on the sports-drink scene is lactate, a non-acidic relative of lactic acid. Recent research has shown that lactate is a preferred fuel source of the muscles and has a buffering effect on the acids produced during intense, anaerobic movements. If such a buffering effect is noticeable, then Cytomax (the first product to employ this technology) would be the sports drink of choice for climbers.

Uses of Sports Drinks

Increased Endurance

Carbohydrate (glycogen) depletion in the muscles and liver is a primary cause of fatigue when performing long-duration activities of more than 90 minutes. The traditional use of sports drinks is for situations when additional fuel means prolonged activity. Your climbing performance on a multi-pitch route or a long day at the crags would benefit from consuming a sports drink in addition to water. Oppositely, an hour or two of climbing or a short gym workout may not benefit from the added fuel, assuming you have normal glycogen reserves, so you would do just fine drinking water and saving some calories.

Faster Recovery

A key factor relating to speed of muscle recovery is the timing of carbohydrate consumption. As Barbara Branda Turner mentioned earlier, the first 15 minutes to two hours following exercise is when your body most quickly stores carbohydrate as muscle glycogen. Unfortunately, a day of climbing is often followed by fasting during the period of time it takes to get back to camp and cook or travel to a restaurant. It's now that you're depriving your body of carbos when it wants them the most. This may be the best reason to start using sports drinks.

The faster you replace your glycogen stores, the more energy you'll have the next day. Furthermore, a large meal eaten several hours after climbing not only stores glycogen more slowly but may also store some of the food as fat. Get into the habit of drinking 50 to 100 grams of carbos as soon as possible after climbing. When you get around to eating dinner, don't pig out!

Improved Anaerobic Performance

A sports drink containing carbos in the form of lactates may be useful in improving anaerobic performance (short powerful exercises or sequences) because of its buffering effect on lactic acid. Although it is uncertain to what extent buffering takes place, even a small increase in performance over normal could mean the difference between flashing a route or falling. Again, Cytomax is the only drink I know that contains lactates.

Electrolyte Replacement

Big wall and alpine climbers would benefit from both the fuel and electrolytes contained in sports drinks. As mentioned earlier, electrolyte loss is slow and easily replaceable through normal food consumption. Only climbers surviving on small meals would significantly benefit from additional electrolytes.

Performance stimulating effects are available through safe, legal products.

Mark Guider photo

SPORTS DRINK COMPARISON

Product	Calories	Carb	Carb Source	Electrolytes
Endura	120/16oz	30 grams	fructose	yes
Exceed Energy Drink	140/16oz	34 grams	glucose polymers	yes
Exceed High Carbo	470/16oz	118 grams	sucrose/glucose	no
Cytomax	150/16oz	40 grams	fructose/polylactate	yes
Carbo Force	400/16oz	100 grams	fructose/glucose	yes
Gatorade	100/16oz	28 grams	sucrose/glucose	yes

Stimulating Performance

Athletes have long been interested in any ergogenic product billed to be a stimulant. Although some people have undoubtedly partaken of illegal stimulants to enhance performance, it is the handful of safe, legal, and scientifically-proven products that should be of interest to climbers. Only three products pass this test: caffeine and the herbs ginseng and ephedra. Forget the rest!

Caffeine – More Than An Energy Boost

Caffeine is the number one ergogenic aid of the common man and athletes alike. It's caffeine's well-documented effects on the central nervous system (CNS) that help you wake up in the morning and become a bit more powerful at the gym or the crags. But caffeine has two lesser known effects that you should know about: increased thermogenesis and glycogen sparing.

Burn More Calories

Thermogenesis is the process by which the body turns calories into heat instead of storing them as body fat. Caffeine has been shown to stimulate thermogenesis resulting in higher calorie utilization. This effect is of particular interest to persons who need a little extra help in dropping those last few pounds of unwanted fat. In fact, some of the early supermarket diet pills were simply caffeine tablets.

Increase Your Endurance

Glycogen is your main source of energy when climbing. Thus if you could somehow extend the length of time your glycogen reserves would last you could climb or train longer. Caffeine does just that. It releases fatty acids into your blood stream for fuel resulting in a slower use of glycogen. Dozens of studies have shown this effect will allow you to exercise harder and longer.

The Bad News

The effects of caffeine are dose dependent. To get the desired effect on a daily basis you'll have to take more and more. That explains why religious one-cup-per-morning coffee drinkers in time turn into three or more cups per morning drinkers – they need more and more to get the same effect.

If you fit into this group, you may actually benefit by cutting back on your coffee on climbing days. Whether you are aware of it or not, large doses of caffeine make you jittery and anxious, feelings you definitely don't want when attempting a delicate face route. Consequently, only non- or occasional coffee drinkers will benefit significantly from drinking a cup or two before climbing.

At the Gym...Okay

The negative effects of caffeine are less critical at the gym. Caffeine's energizing and endurance-enhancing effects are just what the doctor ordered for those long, burning sessions in your home gym. Even after a long day at work, a shot of caffeine might be just what it takes to raise your energy levels enough for a decent gym workout. Remember that caffeine is a diuretic so you'll want to drink plenty of water throughout your workout.

Ginseng

Although this herb has been in use in China for over 5,000 years, the scientific community has only recently begun to explore its possible benefits. A number of studies have shown ginseng to be a weak CNS although its effects are probably less noticeable than caffeine.

Of greater interest are Swiss and Soviet double-blind studies showing increased endurance in athletes on a regular regimen of concentrated ginseng. The Soviet study revealed significant improvement in ten-mile race times of elite runners, although the exact mechanism is not completely understood.

Doses

If you plan to experiment with ginseng it's suggested you take 100-200mg a day for at least 30 days to experience noticeable effects. Unlike caffeine the herb has minimal side effects, although some persons may experience some insomnia and irritability.

This is the bottom line on ginseng: the stimulant properties are not as great as coffee; however, ginseng's endurance-enhancing effects may be of some value for athletes who are already well-tuned. Be aware that these effects may not be noticeable for lesser-trained persons. (For a free research brochure: SunSource Health Products/Ginsana USA, 535 Lipoa Parkway, Suite 110, Kihei, HI 96793)

Ephedra

The ephedra herb, or as the Chinese call it Ma Huang, is simply the most effective supplement I've come across. It is legal and now available in the United States in a capsule form suitable for consumption by athletes.

Ephedrine, the chemical of interest in ephedra (also found in some OTC cold formulas), is a CNS stimulant and bronchial dilator. Its ergogenic effects include increased concentration, intensity, and strength. You will feel these effects from day one!

Although these effects sound similar to those of caffeine, ephedra is a much more powerful ergogenic aid for most, because ephedra is not habitually consumed by the population. The daily consumption of caffeine "spoils" its use as a significant ergogenic aid. This is also the reason ephedrine is now banned at some international athletic competitions.

When taken 30 minutes before a workout, the ephedra herb will fire you up to crank harder, longer, and on smaller holds. More intense workouts over the course of time should result in faster gains in strength.

In addition, a recent study published in the American Journal of Clinical Nutrition (1992;55:246S) reports that ephedra is also thermogenic. As with caffeine, this means it's useful as a training aid in burning extra calories and reducing unwanted fat.

As you might suspect, the side effects of ephedra are similar to those of caffeine: jitters, elevated heart rate, and in a few cases heart palpitations. (As with caffeine, ephedra should not be used by people with heart conditions.) Consequently, ephedra is best used as an aid when training for power, not as a climbing supplement. The exception may be when attempting short powerful climbs or boulder problems. (For addition information on ephedra send a SASE to: Ephedra Info, Box 8633, Lancaster, PA 17604)

Injury Case Studies

The challenge is not only to pursue excellence but to do so without destroying the rest of your life.

Terry Orlick

This chapter contains three case studies invented by Dr. Mark Robinson in a valiant attempt to curb the proliferation of climbing related injuries. They are based on elements of actual cases from his orthopedic practice in Ventura, California, as well as on climbers he has known, and relevant medical literature. These case studies should not be used to replace or avoid proper care by a trained and licensed professional.

I should point out that Dr. Robinson is living proof that modest climbing (and surfing) success can come to those lacking flexibility, fitness, and thinness. Although he appears annually at a number of exotic climbing areas, he is mainly restricted to a sad and lackluster version of blocked practice on dusty glue-ups in Hobo Jungle near Ventura. One of the hobos recently reeled out of the brush, relieved himself on the wall, watched Dr. Robinson climb, and issued the judgment, "You sure don't climb like Lynn Hill. She's pretty good."

TAKING CHANCES

Mark Robinson, M.D.

Patient:

Huck Ammowe, famous boulderer, age 25.

Clinical History:

Huck had been working on the undone problem Hoota-doob on the Jumbo Mumbo boulder for years. This year he delayed his return to graduate school for a week to work on it. He was able to do the famous final move – a four-point double-dyno – from a step ladder, but the first move off the ground continued to elude him and everybody else, too.

On the last possible day before he had to leave, every-thing was right: the light, the humidity, his bio-rhythms and psychological state. He had trained hard, had a good night's sleep, and his minibus was running well. He even had a sweet roll for breakfast.

On his initial try he succeeded on the first move! But as he shifted up toward the final moves there was a momentary

(page opposite)
Mark Robinson, M.D., on a rather exotic route in Oregon.

sway, a microscopic error in movement. He pulled hard and felt a painful pop in his finger. Determined to succeed, he threw all he had into the dyno, a 20 percent proposition from the ladder, and he made it, but not without more grinding noises in his finger.

Back at graduate school he began making the rounds of hand surgeons as he tried to decide what to do. The ascent was mentioned in *Outside* magazine along with a great photo – a sinewy and tense arm, a pained and surprised but still concentrated face.

Commentary:

Beyond a certain point the demands of a climb cannot be reliably met by the climber; success becomes a matter of chance. The precision of movement, the timing and co-ordination of the application of maximum force, the maintenance of confidence in success, or some other demand of the climb, exceed what the human organism can learn to do reliably and repeatedly.

Many games are based on this phenomenon. Archery has evolved now so that hitting the bull's eye is difficult, and splitting the shaft of an arrow in the center of the bull's eye in Robin Hood style is a legendary feat of great skill and even greater luck. Perhaps all of the ultimate boulder problems have this hole-in-one quality. An obvious example is Jim Holloway's "Slapshot." Holloway accomplished this only once, after many attempts, and the feat is still unduplicated.

Some climbers like predictable success – to methodically apply well-practiced techniques and skills that regularly produce a successful ascent. This stay-within-your-limits strategy used to be regarded as the only proper attitude. It is certainly what most sane people like on a big, dangerous route. But in situations where the usual cost of failure is only frustration, most climbers, especially boulderers and sport climbers, prefer to push their limits. Beyond a certain point the demands of a climb cannot be reliably met by the climber and success becomes a matter of chance.

Up to a certain point this demands better technique, concentration, strength, etc. It also makes success more gratifying and shows the climber proof of greater skill and fitness. But beyond that point, different for each person, success is a matter of luck, proof of persistence.

Catastrophic sudden injury occurs quite often in just these situations where physical demands are greatest, the margins for error are all but eliminated, backup mechanisms are impossible, and desire to succeed is great. The desire to push limits into this zone is inevitable in most kinds of climbing, and it is inevitable that injury cannot always be prevented. What's more, intense competition with oneself, or with others, will eventually lead to a level of difficulty that lies beyond the reliable capacity of the biological systems involved.

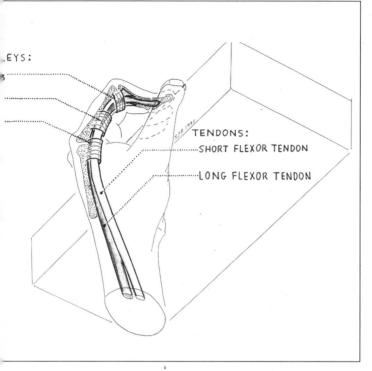

EYS:

TENDONS:

SHORT FLEXOR TENDON

LONG FLEXOR TENDON

The pulleys hold the tendons close to the finger bones. Short flexor tendon connects muscles in the arm to the middle finger bone (phalanx). Long flexor tendon passes through a split in the short flexor tendon to connect to the end (distal) phalanx.

The Story Continues - A2 Again

Back at graduate school, Huck's finger became less painful. Five days after the injury he could type. But because he was concerned, he went to see a hand surgeon with the student health service. The exam showed some tenderness around the middle segment of the finger and the first joint. There was weakness of pinch with the finger against the thumb. This was partially correctable by wrapping tape around the base of the finger. But most important: the tendons on the palm side of the finger seemed to stick out (Bowstring) whenever the finger was bent against a resisting force.

The doctor diagnosed a tear of the A2 Pulley which is one of the guides that holds the tendon against the skeleton of the finger, but the actual tendon itself was intact. He recommended surgical exploration with repair or re-construction of the pulley "because you need full strength for your sport." Huck was willing to go for it but became a bit anxious when he found out that the cost would exceed the amount needed for a new minibus and that extreme climbing would be out for at least several months.

So Huck went to see a second doctor. She made the same diagnosis as the first one – A2-Pulley rupture – but came to the opposite recommendation: no surgery. She said that such an injury was extremely rare, perhaps only seen in climbers – a good guess. She thought that because "natural healing" (the course of healing without effective treatment) was unknown and because surgical treatment could probably be done much later with about the same results, that a "wait-and-see" approach could be taken. It was now about two weeks since the injury, and the bow-string phenomenon was still present. Although it would remain permanently, the tenderness was gone and pinch-strength loss had improved.

Huck resolved this difference of opinion to his own satisfaction by looking up the topic in his school's medical college library. He called the author of one of the articles who told him that many of the world's top competition climbers had suffered such an injury, and all of them regarded it as a curiosity that had no effect on function. Most of the climbers felt that taping the finger was helpful, though.

Six months later Huck got his Ph.D. He packed a ton of tape into his minibus and went on the road looking for jobs and boulders. With consistent, tight taping of the injured finger, he was soon climbing as well as ever. The day after he found a job, the same finger on the other hand blew out, too.

Discussion:

The decision whether or not to have surgery is difficult, especially for athletes. Surgery is expensive and risky. Most orthopedic surgeries involve long recoveries and rehabilitation periods that are onerous for the athlete. Cooperation during this post-surgical period is believed to be important for success, yet athletes are notorious for premature return to sport and for pushing themselves too much and too soon.

A questionnaire sent to a group of climbers by a Los Angeles hand-surgery group found that 50 percent would continue to climb, even if told by a physician that climbing would produce permanent hand damage.

The results of surgical treatment are perhaps not what most athletes expect or desire. Very few professional "throwing" athletes, ever return to their pre-injury level of play after shoulder surgery. Unfortunately, a few high-profile success stories make better copy for newspapers, and so the public comes to have unrealistic expectations.

Surgery is in some ways the artful use of scar tissue to repair or replace a damaged structure, but scar tissue can never acquire the full, desirable properties of the tissue it replaces, so performance after surgery (or any injury for that matter) can improve only if alternative methods of training and execution are employed. These methods must place less stress on the injured parts than those which produced the original injury.

The natural history of many of the new and exotic injuries seen in this era of mass sports obsession are unknown, and how the natural history compares to various new surgical procedures often entirely uninvestigated. Claims about these matters are often merely conjecture or expert opinion. Even common knee-ligament injuries that have been studied for decades have no clearly defined methods of optimum treatment, and there is much controversy about them among surgeons.

The A2-pulley injury– a tendinous tunnel connected to the bones in the finger which prevents the flexor tendon from bowstringing across the finger when it's flexed – is just such an injury. It was created in the anatomy lab by Dr. Marie Duvall in France in the 1980s. She produced a spectrum of injuries from partial pulley tears to complete tearing of the pulley and tendon. She recommended a non-surgical regimen.

Dr. Steve Bollen of Great Britain defined the natural history of the injury to a certain extent in a study of all 67 male competitors at a World Cup event in 1989. He found that 26 percent of these climbers had evidence of an old A2-pulley rupture. None of them regarded it as a problem or impairment and most had learned to tape the injured finger. Dr. Bollen felt that surgical reconstruction was possible but not desirable given the absence of any resumption of climbing too soon after any surgical repair.

French doctor, Y. Tropet, reported on the case of a climber who was treated surgically. This repair was said to be "undoubtedly justified" because of the patient's sport and the presence of weakness five days after injury. The surgical findings were similar to Dr. Duvall's laboratory injuries study. The result was reported as "good" after six months, but climbing status was not reported, nor the climber's resultant strength after the repair. The bowstring was no longer present, though.

Of course, many questions remain. The long-term consequences of this injury are not known and arthritis or tendinitis may result. Whether or not taping can prevent the problem is also unknown, though it seems that it can.

It is not known whether there is permanent loss of strength. Old A2-pulley injuries quite possibly leave some residual effects, even though the World Cup competitors surveyed did not notice any problems. This may be explained by the fact that the hand is a complex and adaptable organ. Climbers at this level are resourceful and highly motivated, so they may have unconsciously learned to bypass any such weakness. In addition, they might not notice a small loss of strength in one tendon of one finger.

Not nearly enough surgery has been done to know how surgical results compare to non-surgical treatment. Consequently, my present conclusion is that surgery is seldom a good choice for an A2-pulley injury. A better treatment would involve time off followed by a slow return to climbing with consistent taping of the injured finger.

Thanks to Jeff Lucas who had a very similar experience to that of the fictional Huck Ammowe. Further readings on this subject include: Hand Injures in Competition Climbers, by S.R. Bollen. British Journal of Sports Medicine, Vol. 24, No. 1, p. 16, 1990; Manual Demands and Consequences of Rock Climbing by K.G. Shea, Journal of Hand Surgery, Vol. 17A, No. 2, p. 200, 1992; Injury to the A2 Pulley in Rock Climbers by S.R. Bollen, Journal of Hand Surgery, Vol. 15B, No. 2, p.268, 1990; Closed Traumatic Rupture of the Ring Finger Flexor Tendon Pulley by Y. Tropet, Journal of Hand Surgery, Vol. 15A, No. 5, p.745, 1990.

The Patient:

R.P., a 22-year-old male, ran track in high school and kept in shape at college by jogging. R.P. regarded himself as "stiff-jointed" (inflexible) but was naturally lean in the style called "skinny-fat" by bodybuilders. He earned a B.A. in Economics and went to work at the Beer Belly Futures Exchange in a large Midwest city.

Clinical History:

R.P. was bored with his job, depressed, and lonely when he met Q.T., a bicycle messenger who had a degree in dance from the same college he attended. Q.T. soon introduced R.P. to climbing at one of the many local climbing gyms.

R.P. liked Q.T., who could top rope hard 5.11, and he wanted to impress her so he began to climb regularly, and besides, it seemed to fill a void in his life. The people at the Exchange also encouraged him. They thought he was a daredevil and liked the way he got all veiny and defined.

Jonathan Houck on a killer move at Morrison, Colorado.

Every night R.P. went to the climbing gym. He warmed up by hanging on a fingerboard until muscle failure or "flash-pump." He then jumped on the hardest route or traverse he thought he could do while still "fresh" and tried it again and again hoping to: (1) impress Q.T.; (2) impress the other climbers and be accepted; (3) experience the joys of self-mastery.

After about six months of this routine, combined with a strict low fat/low calorie diet, R.P. hit a rut. He felt dejected and tired. He had muscle aches and caught colds frequently. R.P.'s morning pulse rate went up, and not even his five- to ten-mile runs every other morning, which he did at the expense of his sleep, seemed to help. His elbows hurt like crazy and he put so much tape on his arms and fingers that people started to call him "the mummy." Still, he could usually on-sight 5.10c and once did a one move 5.11b.

Looking for an answer, R.P. began to see Ms. Nea Dole, an unlicensed, self-proclaimed acupuncturist/natural healer who advertised in the gyms. R.P.'s treatment involved a regime of acupressure, rolfing, shiatsu, and lots of amino acid supplements, particularly L-tryptophan, to treat fatigue and depression and to "realign the mind-body conundrum."

The result of all of this treatment was unpromising for R.P. He experienced arm and leg swelling and numbness, with tingling, icy pains in the hands and feet. This, of course, led to a further decline in climbing performance.

Knowing she was up against a tough problem, Ms. Dole doubled the L-tryptophan dose. Still, no improvement seemed apparent to R.P., not even with the exertion of superhuman willpower and even more training.

At this point, a concerned co-worker convinced R.P. to see a doctor, a man specializing in "sports medicine, diets, executive wellness, laser hemorrhoid treatment, and liposuction." This doctor diagnosed Carpal Tunnel Syndrome and suggested office surgery. Unfortunately, the surgical wound became infected and wouldn't heal, and now R.P. couldn't climb at all.

In desperation, R.P. decided on his own to again double the dose of L-tryptophan. Soon after he collapsed at work and was admitted to University Hospital. About two weeks later he died in intensive care of "Ascending Polyneuropathy, Sepsis, and Multiple Organ Failure." Investigators from The Center for Disease Control in Atlanta reviewed his records months later.

Commentary:

It is still possible to get killed climbing, even if you never touch a real cliff or mountain. What's more, this poor patient never made a right decision in his entire climbing career. In fact, he climbed for all the wrong reasons: to impress people and look good.

At the gym, his warm-up was too severe and too rapid, and he trained daily, which was far too often, thereby depriving his body of time to adapt and build new tissue. As with all new climbers, it would have been better for him to begin training in flexibility, technique, body control, and energy conservation. Instead, he worked on strength, power, energy squandering big moves, and attempting to tick the high grades. To top things off, R.P. dieted severely all the while, depriving himself of the nutrients necessary to rebuild and recharge.

Predictably, R.P. sustained localized overuse injuries including medial elbow tendinosis and chronic tearing of the finger tendons and associated structures because his muscles and desire grew faster than the more slowly adapting ligaments and tendons. R.P. also suffered from a systemic 'overtraining' syndrome resulting in fatigue, muscle aches, depressed immune system, elevated morning heart rate, etc. He should have taken about two months off and seen a sports medicine specialist. Instead, he trained more and went to a quack.

From the now illegal amino-acid supplement L-tryptophan he got the Eosinophilia-Myalgia Syndrome (EMS) which gave him swelling, nerve damage, and exhaustion. This was misdiagnosed as carpal tunnel syndrome on the basis of a quick and superficial analysis (crazy climber type, job at keyboard, numb fingers = carpal tunnel syndrome) leading to unnecessary and complicated surgery. He became one of the 25 or so people to have died of EMS before its cause, L-tryptophan, was restricted by the FDA.

Postscript

This case had a gruesome aftermath. R.P.'s parents knew that he'd wanted his ashes spread over his favorite cliff. Unfortunately, they didn't know anything about climbing, so they asked Ms. Q.T. to arrange this. She was in a quandary, though, because as far as she knew, all of his climbing was done indoors. Gym owners certainly would not want his ashes dumped around their establishments, and Devil's Lake, the only crag she'd been to, seemed inappropriate because of its name.

In desperation, Q.T. finally bought a large amount of chalk, mixed the ashes in with it and gave it away at various gyms. Thus were his ashes spread over many a gym and crag and concentrated on hard "killer" moves. Ms. Dole even took some to cut her dwindling, but still saleable, stock of L-tryptophan.

YOUTHFUL ENTHUSIASM

The Patient:

A young male about 14 years of age with exaggerated muscle development and considerable subcutaneous fat.

Clinical History:

The patient was inspired to become a rock climber at the age of 11 when exposed to a "Constant Sports Network" show about master solo climber Duane Arley. He appreciated two facts: climbing takes strength; and climbers are light and wiry. He began to train a lot, usually in bodybuilding gyms. The local gurus there put him on a high-protein diet.

Most of his climbing experience was on short, severely overhanging boulders which he would ascend using very powerful sequences. He noticed, though, that experienced climbers rarely seemed to do those problems the same way he did, nor did they have as much difficulty. Still, he continued to progress but became bulky and not appreciably less fat looking. He wanted me to prescribe "the kind of steroids that make you whippet thin but strong as an ox."

He also had knee pain which began while doing squats, an alleged way to develop total body power and coordination. His legs were large but with small, high-riding knee caps. X-rays of his knees showed the growth plates were still open (i.e. his bones had not reached full length). Also, his medial quadriceps were underdeveloped as compared to his lateral quads.

I declined to prescribe steroids explaining that they are illegal and would lead to growth arrest and numerous complications including acne. I advised eating a regular healthy diet, leaving the bodybuilding gym, adding aerobic exercise, and doing some moderate-intensity endurance climbing. For his knee I suggested leg extensions in the last few degrees of knee extension.

This advice was so far from what he had come to expect after years of exposure to sports TV and body-building mags that he was unlikely to believe it.

Commentary:

As climbing becomes more popular and more widely exposed in mainstream sources, it will predictably inspire physically immature people. High-performance climbers now come as young as seven years of age. Climbing is probably harmless and even natural for children until it reaches the point of competition, obsession, or involves "stage" parents. Until skeletal maturity, it is best to allow all childhood sports to remain at the level of self-regulated "play," rather than the adult forms of self-discipline and goal-directed performance maximization. This is where the rich field of unique overuse pathologies begins, which involves the destruction of growing joints as seen in the classic case of little-leaguer's elbow. Interestingly, this patient never developed the hand/elbow/shoulder versions of these problems seen in many climbers but rather a weightlifting-related problem which is common and relatively easy to treat.

I will spare you lectures about the evils of anabolic steroids. However, there is one definitive point: steroids are useful only to increase muscle mass, perhaps by allowing what would otherwise be overtraining. In climbing, muscle mass is probably nearly irrelevant – take a look at the stars – and most of what is required can generally be obtained from climbing, along with a normal endocrine (hormone) system.

The author's five-year-old niece, Simone Hörst, displays her own brand of youthful enthusiasm!

For me, the main lesson of this case is the demonstration of the poor level of general knowledge that people have available in their usual surroundings to help them achieve sports goals. For most people, "climb well" = "train a lot + diet," and "training" = "weightlifting." Weightlifting has its own traditions and ideas, some of which are not true. These were developed mostly for bodybuilding and contact sports and do not carry over well to climbing.

There are books that recommend squats and other power-lifting techniques for climbers. The rationale for these exercises rests on such murky concepts as coordination or total body power. In fact, the ideas contained in these concepts are quite probably wrong. Squats will result in overly bulky legs that become excess baggage and place extra weight on the arms in most vertical and overhanging climbing situations. Further, doing squats teaches you the coordination of doing squats and nothing more.

Studies in "Motor Skills and Learning" indicate that coordination in one activity transfers little, if any, to other seemingly similar activities. For the purposes of our sport, this means that climbing is the only way to develop climbing coordination. Walking on slack chain will improve your slack chain walking ability but not your climbing balance. Hanging with your feet dangling will improve your dangling endurance, but will be of little help to your climbing ability with your feet on the rock. Pull-ups will add strength to your pull muscles, but do nothing to help your climbing technique unless your plan is to keep sneaking peeks at a bird's nest on a ledge above a roof!

Of course, weightlifting will add some strength, and this can help some climbers who have good techniques but lack strength. In addition, some weightlifting is helpful to balance the muscular overdevelopment that can result from climbing. But too much strength too early can lead to bad technique since energetically inefficient moves can be used to bypass the crucial step of learning efficient climbing movements.

Author Eric Hörst circa 1980, in his "younger" days, on "Bonnie's Roof" (5.9), Shawangunks, New York.

Ed Park photo

Finally, the patient fell into the old bodybuilding tradition of protein cultism, which can actually be counterproductive. Many protein foods are high in fat, and only so much protein can be absorbed anyway. Climbers do not need to have any particular weight, rather they need to minimize their weight in areas not used for climbing. This involves reduction of body fat and unnecessary muscle mass in the legs. A tricky balance between mass and endurance must be struck with the arms and shoulders.

Aftermath:

This poor lad never did become a big name solo climber. He ignored my advice and slandered me at the gym. Eventually he did get lots of steroids from the black market and at about age 17 came before a judge because of some bad behavior. This occurred due to the triple psychological strains of "roid rage" or steroid-induced aggressive behavior), rejection by girls for acne and brutish behavior, and pain produced by hemorrhoids due to heavy squats. As part of a crackdown on drugs, he was sentenced to six months at the Honor Rancho. As luck had it, this one was in the California Sierras near some excellent boulders. Numerous escape attempts to go bouldering led to longer sentences and eventually time in an adult penitentiary. This all led to a life of crime. Ironically he did get to meet his hero Duane Arley – they shared a cell one night after Duane punched out a rap bolter.

Home Gym

If we all did the things we are capable of doing, we would literally astound ourselves.

Thomas A. Edison

For many climbers "indoor training" refers, not to climbing gym workouts, but to crank sessions put in at a home gym. Although generally small in size, such home gyms can be extremely effective, particularly because of their convenience. Training at home eliminates travel time, and it allows you to do other things while resting between burns. So if lack of time has been keeping you from the rock, then bring the "rock" to you!

In this chapter you'll be introduced to four different kinds of home gyms, from a $2,000 adjustable-angle wall to a $75 finger-training woodie. No matter the amount of space and money you have available, you could be climbing at home in a matter of hours or days.

Stop thinking about it, and start doing it. The plans on the following pages will see you on your way, and by all means, ad-lib at will.

HOUSE OF PAIN

Todd Skinner

The core of every good training program involves lots of bouldering. Consequently, if you don't have a crag or gym nearby, or if winter weather has set in, then consider building a bouldering room.

My bouldering room has hundreds of permanent (yes, permanent) holds and is centered around a 12-foot-by-12-foot, 60-degree past vertical wall with 80 percent wooden holds and 20 percent Yaniro pockets. Every hold has a name. This lets me avoid aimless movement, and it facilitates the recording of boulder problems. The room was designed and built by Brian Pederson, a Wisconsin climber who also designed, built, and owns the largest private gym in the U.S that is known as the "Barn."

Two views of Todd Skinner's personal "House of Pain," the bouldering wall in his home in Lander, Wyoming.

My entire gym was built in two caffeine-fueled days and nights. The highlight of the effort came when Brian, exhausted and strung out on coffee, locked back the guard on the power saw at about 2:30 a.m. of the second day and began using the saw as a freestyle planer. (Do not try this!) The rest of the crew bolted for the door, but the result was an outstanding bouldering room!

(page opposite)

Top U.S. sport climber, Jim Karn, trains even while hauling around a cast on his right leg.

Chris Goplerud photo

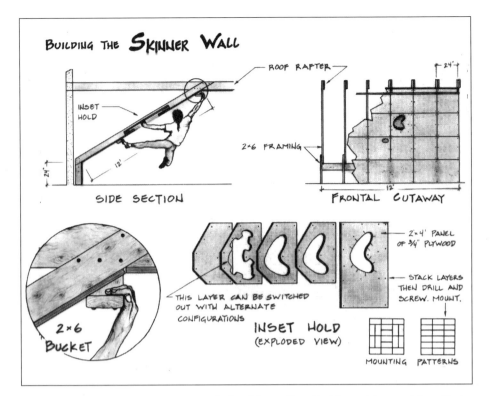

BUILDING THE SKINNER WALL

ROOF RAFTER

INSET HOLD

2×6 FRAMING

24"

24"

12'

SIDE SECTION

FRONTAL CUTAWAY

12'

2×6 BUCKET

THIS LAYER CAN BE SWITCHED OUT WITH ALTERNATE CONFIGURATIONS

2×4' PANEL OF ¾" PLYWOOD

STACK LAYERS THEN DRILL AND SCREW. MOUNT.

INSET HOLD (EXPLODED VIEW)

MOUNTING PATTERNS

I should mention that I went to great trouble to make sure my bouldering room was well-insulated, well-lit, and fully carpeted – an attractive destination! Not only am I drawn to spend more time in it, but it's easier to recruit other climbers for added energy and enthusiasm.

The Theory

For the steep, vogue routes of the '90s, power means EVERYTHING! If you have the power to do the moves on a route, you have a good chance of bagging it. Stamina and technique are important, however, it often comes down to raw power so you'd better train accordingly!

The best way to build applicable power is to concentrate on short, brutal boulder problems. I view my steepest training wall not as an indoor wall but as an actual boulder. The goal is to create explosive, intensely powerful routes, lasting no longer than 15 seconds, that have definite starting and ending points – usually a bucket at the top of the wall. This approach reinforces the mind set that a boulder problem is a finite event and that laser-like focus and concentration must be maintained until the event is over.

The permanence of the holds is twofold. First, like a real boulder, the problems on the wall should evolve over months and years. With time, sequences will be born that you would have never imagined earlier on. Second, it takes a lot of time to link-up, or perform in sequence, many of your hardest problems. Only by doing this can you simulate the hardest routes at the crags – routes that possess many desperate boulder problems that may take months or years to do!

The Workout

We usually spend about an hour warming up prior to trying the hardest problems. When we're ready to begin serious bouldering, we apply the same approach used at a real boulder. Each climber takes a turn, and only one climber is on the wall at a time. Every problem is defined by which hand hits which holds and what your feet can or cannot use to help. The session gets progressively more savage until 80 percent of the problems are being done "campus style" (without feet) – definitely not a beginner's routine!

The full workout takes several hours but is typically followed by two full days off. Also, don't forget to reinforce your finger tendons with tape before partaking in such a savage power workout. And remember: play hard, dream wildly, shoot straight, and train like tomorrow might never come!

HOUSE OF STYLE

Russ Clune finishing a traverse of his 32-foot - wide adjustable wall.

Build an Adjustable Indoor Wall
Russ Clune

Face it. No matter where you live, quality climbing time on the crags is going to be hampered by bad weather.

In the earlier days of youthful enthusiasm I'd go up to the Gunks regardless of what Mother Nature was up to. Now being older and wiser, and with readily available manufactured holds, it's obvious that an indoor climbing wall is a better choice. A wall at home guarantees a fun and pumping workout in a controlled environment at any time of the day or night.

I had a bay of a two-car garage to work with. Marty Trumbauer, a local carpenter and climber, and I focused on designing a wall that could change angles. Marty came upon a simple and elegant solution: clothesline adjusters. This design allows for each panel to be adjusted individually and in a matter of seconds.

Besides adjustability, another key to not becoming bored with the wall is holds – have lots of them. We have t-nuts inserted on an 8-inch grid system. If it were being done again,

---

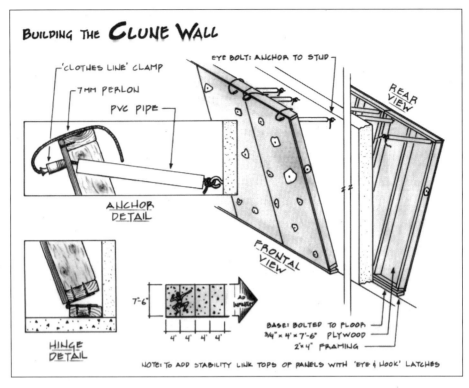

BUILDING THE CLUNE WALL

'CLOTHES LINE' CLAMP

7MM PERLON

PVC PIPE

EYE BOLT: ANCHOR TO STUD

REAR VIEW

ANCHOR DETAIL

HINGE DETAIL

FRONTAL VIEW

7'-6"

4' 4' 4' 4'

BASE: BOLTED TO FLOOR
3/4" × 4' × 7'-6" PLYWOOD
2"× 4" FRAMING

NOTE: TO ADD STABILITY LINK TOPS OF PANELS WITH 'EYE & HOOK' LATCHES

I'd have even more. You can't have too many holds! We have over 700 on ours, and I still buy more.

In the end, what you build will be determined by the space you have. We had about 375 square feet of floor space to work with and ended up with 760 square feet of wall broken into 300 square feet of adjustable traversing wall, 300 square feet of horizontal roof, 100 square feet of vertical wall,

The House of Style, Russ Clune's home gym.

and 60 square feet of 135-degree wall. The only thing we'd like to have is more height.

Use your space wisely and spend plenty of time planning before you start building. It's a good idea to talk to some people who have a wall to find out what they like and dislike. By the same token, don't be afraid to experiment and invent because you might come up with a better set-up than we have.

Death Board – Campus Board

First introduced by Tony Yaniro in the 1984 video On The Rocks, the Death Board, or "machine" as it was then called, became a staple exercise for a few of California's strongest climbers. Surprisingly, this device has never become widely adopted even thought it's both builder- and user-friendly and extremely sport specific. Maybe it was the name...

The Death Board simply consists of a 16-foot plank onto which horizontal wooden strips are screwed for handholds. The Board is most often used outside where it can be leaned against a tree branch and worked at varying angles, although a shorter eight-foot version often referred to as a campus board, can be built for indoor use. By design the wooden handholds are very positive and well sanded to make them as painless and easy to grip as possible. This is critical because you will be using the Death Board at steep angles (120 to 130 degrees is preferred), and you will be doing many, many laps!

Furthermore, I suggest that you add few, if any, modular holds to the Death Board – save them for a climbing wall. The objective here is to perform simple, yet powerful, movements that delve deep into the forearm muscles, not to sharpen your ability to sequence or grab irregularly-shaped holds. You should be able to turn off your brain when working the board. Your complete focus should be placed on pumping another lap and hanging on a little bit longer.

As you see, the only death this board will bring is the "death of forearm weakness!" Beginner and intermediate climbers can use it to improve forearm endurance, and expert climbers can build radical finger power as well as more endurance. So get busy!

Building an Adjustable-Angle Wall

1.) Bolt 2x4s to the floor along the base of the wall.

2.) If your garage has a standard eight-foot ceiling, you will need to cut a few inches of length off each plywood sheet to allow for a proper fit (due to floor-board).

3.) Begin framing the plywood sheets as shown above. Use two-inch drywall screws at one-foot intervals.

4.) Drill t-nut holes in the plywood every eight inches or in a random pattern if you like. Then hammer on the t-nuts on the back of the board.

5.) Drill a 3/8-inch hole in the top two corners of each ply-wood panel for the perlon cord.

6.) Lay the finished panels side by side and face down along the floor board.

7.) Attach piano hinges to the 2x4 at the bottom of each plywood panel, then to the floor board.

8.) Anchor an eye bolt to the garage wall studs about six inches below the ceiling.

9.) Tie a three-foot length of 7mm perlon to the eye bolt.

10.) Lift up the panels and thread the other end of the perlon through the appropriate hole and fasten with a clothesline adjuster.

11.) Mount your modular holds and get climbing!

Additional notes: For added stability you can add "eye & hook" latches to snap adjacent panels together. If you plan to use wall mostly at one angle, you can also add an appropriate length of PVC pipe on each perlon cord to prevent any minor bouncing of panel that may occur.

BUILDING A DEATH BOARD

Strip Preparation

1) Cut 10 small strips (1 inch) and 10 large strips (2 inch) to the width of the board.

2) Trim 30 degrees and sand one edge of each strip to provide a positive grip.

Mounting Strips and Drilling Pockets

1) Mount strips at 16-inch intervals with self-driving drywall screws and glue (PL-400 sub-floor glue is best).

2) Mount small holds from the bottom. Mount large holds starting about 7 feet from the bottom.

3) Drill 2- and 3-finger pockets at 16-inch intervals. These should be at least 1-inch deep and well rounded.

Mounting Stiffener Board

1) Screw a 16-foot 2x4 on edge to the back of the Death Board.

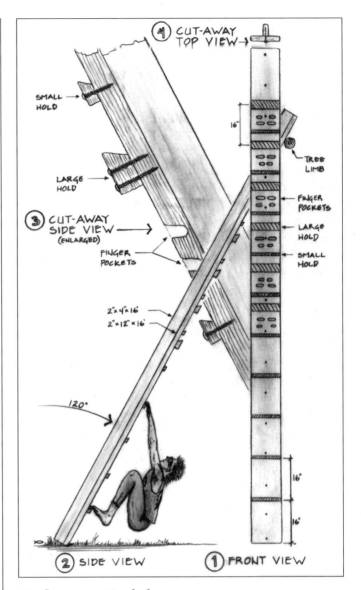

④ CUT-AWAY TOP VIEW

SMALL HOLD

LARGE HOLD

16"

TREE LIMB

FINGER POCKETS

LARGE HOLD

SMALL HOLD

③ CUT-AWAY SIDE VIEW (ENLARGED)

FINGER POCKETS

2"x4"x16'
2"x12"x16'

120°

16"

16"

② SIDE VIEW

① FRONT VIEW

Endurance Training

As usual, begin with a 10- to 15-minute warm-up consisting of some pull-ups, warm-up laps (big holds only), stretches, and Sportsmassage. The body of your workout will be three all-out burns to failure separated by a 10-minute rest. For each of these burns, your goal is to climb up and down the board (a lap) for as long as possible. Use a watch to measure the length of each burn, because time is a better measure of fitness than the number of laps.

Beginner and intermediate climbers should start on the small strips, while advanced persons can use the pockets. Move up and down the board using only the size of hold you chose. You may want to begin with the crimp grip and switch to the stronger open-hand grip as you begin to tire. Place your feet on the small strips only, and forget climbing shoes, sneakers work just fine.

Continue with as many laps on your chosen size hold as possible. Mix up your sequence by "matching" (hand matching on each hold), "alternating" (as in climbing a ladder), and "skipping" (using every other small strip) handholds. When you can no longer hang onto the small strip, move to the larger holds. Continue in the same manner but now grab only the larger holds with feet still on the small strip only.

Finish each lap with a good shakeout and chalk while hanging on the lowest large strip. Your goal is to recoup some of your lost energy. Work on finding foot arrangements and hip positions on the small strips near the bottom of the board that provide the most efficient rests. These shakeouts will also educate you on the degree to which you can recover while in a similar position on a route.

As fatigue increases, you'll learn to race through each lap in an attempt to get back to the rest position before you pump out. This is the "zone" that results in the greatest physical gains, so hang on! These last few laps will also improve your mental fortitude because you will learn to climb on through the increased discomfort of a sickening pump.

Finally, you'll reach muscular failure and need to step off the board and "detox." Take care not to reach failure while near the top of the board. When in doubt, work half laps as you approach muscular failure. Take note of the elapsed time of your first set or burn. Rest for 10 minutes or so, then move onto the second of your three prescribed burns.

Power Training – A Campus Workout

The best gains in power always result from short, intense bursts of work. This is achieved on the Death Board by powering up the board with no feet, or what is also known as campusing. This is an advanced exercise that requires significant base strength. If you cannot do the prerequisite 20 pull-ups or a solid one-arm lock-off, then hold off on this variation of the exercise. If you pass the "test," be sure to warm-up well, and tape the first joint of your fingers before you begin.

As in endurance training, begin with the small holds for the initial laps. Power up the board using only your hands then come down with the aid of your feet for safety. Due to the intense nature of this exercise, most users step off and rest at the end of one lap. Rest for several minutes between sets. Your long-term goal is to build up to 10 sets.

As with any new exercise, you'll want to add this to your regimen gradually. Start with once a week, then move to twice a week as long as no unusual pangs develop. Don't forget, always reinforce your tendon pulleys with tape as a precaution, and take a few weeks off from this exercise at the first sign of an injury.

Finding a good location for the Death Board may be the most difficult step. Leaning it against a support beam in a high garage is ideal; a tall tree with a big branch is most common. Check out the backyards of your friends and neighbors. When you find a good tree, tie the top of the board in place so it doesn't move while being used or become airborne during the next wind storm! Enjoy and get pumpin'.

THE WOODIE

This small, yet effective, training woodie will be of interest if you live in an apartment. No longer will the lack of a garage or basement prevent you from performing sport-specific training at home because this finger-training woodie can be built anywhere! Best of all, it's free-standing, so you won't have to damage the apartment walls or ceiling and then face the wrath of your landlord!

The woodie shown below is much more than a hang-board. This device will provide you with tendon-forgiving, endurance-building movements for the fingers, arms, and back that are similar to those found on steep rock.

To use this woodie place your toes on a crate or step ladder spaced several feet behind the structure. Starting with both hands on the low board, alternate hand movements up and down between the two levels of holds. Control the intensity of the exercise by moving the foothold toward or away from the board. Your goal is to perform several long burns of four to 10 minutes, each separated by 10 to 15 minute rests. In addition to building endurance, you will

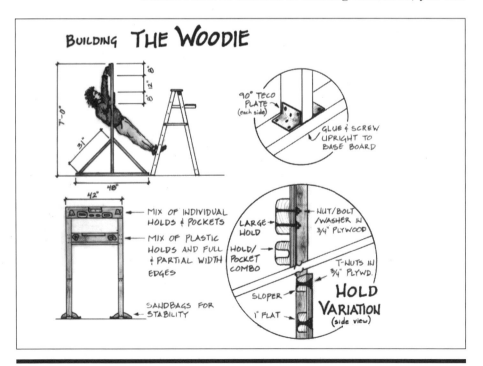

BUILDING THE WOODIE

7'-0"

12" 8" 8"

3'

42" 48"

90° TECO PLATE (each side)

GLUE & SCREW UPRIGHT TO BASE BOARD

MIX OF INDIVIDUAL HOLDS & POCKETS

MIX OF PLASTIC HOLDS AND FULL & PARTIAL WIDTH EDGES

SANDBAGS FOR STABILITY

LARGE HOLD

HOLD/ POCKET COMBO

SLOPER

1" FLAT

NUT/BOLT /WASHER IN 3/4" PLYWOOD

T-NUTS IN 3/4" PLYWD.

HOLD VARIATION (side view)

learn to rest in overhanging positions, practice an occasional deadpoint, and develop the mental fortitude to hang on through increasing muscular discomfort!

Building the Woodie

Construction of this apparatus takes only a few hours of labor and a modest sum of money. You don't even need to purchase a traditional fingerboard to attach – they are generally too painful on your skin to use for repeatedly long burns. Homemade wooden holds are arguably the best. In fact, some of Europe's top climbers swear by wooden-hold training because it allows them to train longer and harder.

First fabricate the two horizontals that will serve as your handholds. As mentioned a variety of wooden holds screwed and glued to the .75 inch plywood is best. Use mostly blocks of wood that are about the size of a deck of cards. Small holds should be .75 inch deep with large holds about 1.5 inches in depth. Vary the width of the holds so as to make two, three, and four finger holds.

Also make two pinch holds for each board. Trapezoid shaped blocks (3 inches across the top and 4.5 inches across the bottom) work best. You will want to make a good bucket hold at the top of each board, as well as drill a few two- and three-finger pockets.

Sand and sculpt all the holds to eliminate sharp, painful edges. If you like, add a few commercial modular holds to the horizontals. Since these holds are rotatable, they offer additional variety. Use 80-grit sandpaper later to rough up the holds if they get greasy from extended use.

Once you have cut all the large pieces, find a partner to hold the supports while you fire in the screws. Squirt a moderate amount of Elmer's glue into each joint as you screw it shut. This significantly reduces any sway you might experience when using the woodie. Allow your woodie 24 hours to dry before use. Also, something heavy like a 25 pound weight or pack placed on the floorboards will help steady your woodie when you make quick movements.

Remember, this device is to train endurance, not power. Try to make each burn last the length of one or two songs, then take a two or three song rest. Always use your feet to support a portion of your weight. Try to become aware of how shifting your weight affects your movements and rests. Work rapid sequences, slow cranks, straight-arm rests, etc. Use your imagination and go for a sick pump!

Supplies Needed to Build the Woodie

Four - 2x4s by 10 feet; kiln dried. If you weigh more than 160 pounds substitute:

Two - 4x4s for the vertical supports

25 3-inch drywall screws for connecting the 2x4s

25 - 1.5-inch drywall screws for attaching the horizontals and Teco plate

Four - 90 degree Teco plates

Two - pieces of 3/4-inch plywood for the horizontals (approximately. 8" x 42")

One - bottle of Elmer's glue.

Training Interviews

CHAPTER 8

What you can do, or dream you can do,
Begin it,
Boldness has genius, power and magic
In it.

Goethe

John Gill, Lynn Hill, Kurt Smith, and Mia Axon are people I have enjoyed talking to. They are all truly nice people and each possesses a deep love for climbing.

Interestingly, they all have a different personal focus at which they have excelled in this sport. Notice that in each of them, there are similarities in attitude but uniqueness in execution. It is these things that set them apart from the masses and made them great climbers.

I hope you find their words as valuable and inspirational as I have. Study, and maybe even model, the beliefs and attitudes they employ in their pursuit of excellence. Risk enlightenment! It takes but a single new idea to change yourself and your climbing.

JOHN GILL – MASTER OF ROCK

Too many young upstarts don't know who John Gill is. What a shame. Todd Skinner and I agree that he was a hero for our generation, which began climbing in the late '70s. It was his ideas and outrageous boulder problems that inspired us all to begin training for climbing in the first place.

John Gill is the Father of Training for Climbing. His feats of strength both on and off the rock have become legendary, but for me his boulder problems are the most amazing thing. By today's grading scale many of them certainly contain 5.12 moves or harder – an accomplishment that, in relative terms, may never be equaled considering that the highest standard in those days was 5.10+/5.11!

FLASH: How old were you when you started climbing? Were you already involved in gymnastics or did you begin training specifically for climbing?

GILL: I began climbing in 1953 when I was a junior in high school in Atlanta, Georgia. I was not an athlete at the time, and it was the sense of adventure and daring that I found fascinating. Later, during my freshman year at Georgia Tech, I was introduced to gymnastics and began working the apparatus for the sake of learning artistic gymnastic moves, which appealed to both my aesthetic nature and the hidden athlete in me and as conditioning for rock climbing.

(page opposite)

John Gill in flight on "The Fatted Calf", (dynamic variation), Pueblo, Colorado.

FLASH: Is it true that you became interested in overhanging routes back in 1959? That would put you about 30 years ahead of the rest of the country.

GILL: I became interested in overhanging rock problems around 1957. By that time I was fairly accomplished on the still rings and 20-foot rope climb and loved the sensation of controlled motion executed by the muscles of the upper torso and arms. During the summers of 1958 and 1959, I did what were probably my first fairly difficult dynamic ascents of overhanging boulder routes – including the Red Cross overhang at Jenny Lake. I also did a few 5.10 moves on longer climbs in the Tetons and elsewhere.

FLASH: Clearly, training is necessary to climb overhanging routes. What exercises did you find most useful? What was a typical workout session comprised of?

GILL: Although I did a lot of rope climbing for speed, I don't think that had much carry-over to traditional rock climbing – too much a matter of skill and dynamic technique. To train for the dynamic start seated on the floor, I would do about ten consecutive, fast muscle ups on the high bar. This contributed to my dynamic technique on the rock, I suppose. On the rings I was more interested in learning the top strength moves for their own sake. I had not been an athlete in high school, and it was great fun to do these awesome things that very few others could accomplish. My favorite move was a butterfly mount through an L-cross from a dead hang. At one point I did, I believe, three consecutive butterfly mounts. I also did the standard slow straight-body cross mount, the slow straight body pull to a handstand from a hang, the Azaryin (a triple cross combo), front lever, back lever, and (poor) Maltese cross.

Later, as I moved away from formal gymnastic tricks, I began to develop more specific exercises for climbing. One-arm pull-ups were good for overhanging rock, and a one-arm version of the front lever was a move I had never heard of anyone else doing, but it seemed to be appropriate for climbing. I did squeeze grip pull-ups on beams, pulling into a front lever occasionally, and at one time, on a really rough and slightly warped beam did a momentary one-arm hang with a squeeze grip.

FLASH: Did you ever practice regular two-arm pull-ups, or just one-arms?

GILL: I did the requisite twenty consecutive pull-ups for a grade of "A" in that part of my gymnastic class at Tech. For bouldering, one-arm pull-ups are of more value – power over endurance.

FLASH: Obviously the fingers are the link to the rock and must be trained, too. Unfortunately, forearm gains come so very slowly for most! Was this the case with you, or were your fingers not usually the point of failure when bouldering?

GILL: The fingers are definitely the weak link between climber and severe rock. I seem to have had some natural, latent predisposition toward finger and arm strength. At the end of a gymnastic workout I would pull into a one-arm on a 1/2 -3/4" door jamb and hold it for a moment. That's all it really took. Just a brief attempt every other day. I never pushed too hard.

FLASH: So you did no specific training for the fingers?

GILL: I occasionally squeezed a rubber handball but mostly did what I have just described. I also learned a one-finger pull-up, since someone told me Herman Buhl could do one! I later found out that this claim was unfounded. The one-finger pull-up is more a circus trick than a necessity for climbing. I frequently added body weight on one-arm pull-ups – up to 20 pounds, but only on occasion for finger exercises. The tendons and ligaments there are too delicate for much abuse.

FLASH: Will you briefly describe your training philosophies?

GILL: For years I worked out approximately every other day, resting the body on intervening days. I got too sore if I tried to exercise rigorously each day. Also my commitment drifted a bit if I forced myself to push my limits so often. The every-other-day regimen gave my life more variety. I have always considered the principal value of climbing to be recreational in character – balance to the other aspects of life. When working out, I normally did not push to failure or exhaustion. Each person is unique. You must experiment with your own body to find out what works best for you. Beware the gurus who advocate one training style for all! Part of the great attraction of climbing is its appeal to individuality, its personal nature. For me, climbing has always been a solitary pursuit, even in the company of friends.

FLASH: How do you view warm-up and stretching exercises? Have they always been a part of your workout schedule?

GILL: Here we come to my biggest failure! I've always been "tight," and stretching exercises inevitably produced painful tendons – I simply don't stretch very well! I did the best I could, and, really, I rarely encountered a move on the rock that required yoga-like contortions. That's probably changed by now with higher standards.

FLASH: Many of today's top climbers follow strict diets. Did you adjust your diet for purposes of maximizing training/climbing performance?

GILL: Lots of animal protein and vitamins C and E. For as long as I can recall, I've eaten a can of tuna almost every day for lunch. When I was younger I ate much beef—loved a good steak or prime rib. I eat mostly fish and chicken now. Lower grades of protein leave me with a washed-out feeling and little creative energy. I probably ate too much food earlier in my career as a climber. I weighed 180 pounds for many years, occasionally going as high as 190. That's too heavy for climbing. Although most of that weight was muscle, a lot of it was not required for rock work! Had I been less a glutton, I would have done a bit better than I did.

FLASH: I believe you're now in your mid fifties, and from what I understand you still possess incredible strength by anyone's standards! How often do you currently train/climb?

GILL: I'm 56. When my wife and I moved into our current home on the prairie ten miles west of Pueblo seven years ago, I built a compact "jungle gym" in my garage that I use once or twice a week, both for strength and aerobic conditioning. It consists of a 12' vertical ladder made with 2x4s that I can do laps on, a version that overhangs about 15 degrees, a severely overhanging aluminum ladder along the underside of the roof, a high bar for pull-ups, a pair of metal rings for dips, and assorted wooden and metal ledges fastened to horizontal beams for hand traverses. I can still do a modest one-arm pull-up on a 3/4" ledge if I practice for a day or so. Normally I just do a hand traverse. I can still do a front lever, also. It's still fun to crawl around upside down as a middle-aged spider!

I should point out that when I was fifty I had a bad arm injury in which I pulled the biceps of my right arm away from the bone of the forearm. It was surgically reattached, but the surgeon smiled gently and shook his head when I asked if he thought I would ever do a one arm pull-up again. A year after surgery I could do one! I don't do real bouldering anymore – the biceps that separated were held to the bone primarily by scar tissue, and we surmised that there were probably other weak points in my body after 30 years of severe dynamic moves. Consequently, I have returned to solo climbing on longer, easier routes – a style of climbing I have always enjoyed, from my first solo on the east face of Long's Peak in 1954 through years of illegal soloing in the Tetons, to many enchanting and solitary adventures on obscure domes and granite bastions in Colorado. Now I train to keep fit for this fascinating and strangely spiritual undertaking. The extra upper torso strength provides that feeling of transcendent lightness that lies at the heart of climbing pleasure. Plus, I do an occasional hard move up high in the air.

FLASH: Do you have any suggestions for middle-aged climbers interested in continuing to climb at a reasonably high level?

GILL: My only advice would be to perhaps engage in fewer dynamic moves – tendons and muscles tear more easily in middle age. They should know their body by now and understand the requirements of continued activity. I might suggest he ask himself why he wants to continue tackling difficult problems. There are, after all, a variety of ways to appreciate the climbing experience – difficulty, by itself, narrows the focus too much.

An unexamined climber's life...

FLASH: You became well known for your amazing dynamic sequences; you were also the first climber to adopt the use of gymnastics chalk into climbing. Can you give a brief history of both?

GILL: As I've said, I began dynamics in the mid to later '50s, against the querulous advice of traditionalists, who worshiped the concept of three-point suspension and

John Gill's One-Arm Front Lever. Do not attempt this at home!

abhorred lunging. It was a style that tied in remarkably well with the gymnastics I was learning. And I could see with great clarity that climbing technique and accomplishments could be improved dramatically – if not entirely by me, then at least I could point the way.

In the Tetons in the mid '50s I observed the guide, Dick Pownall, and a ranger named Emerson practicing climbing on what later became known as Cutfinger Rock. They patted their hands in the dry forest duff before trying to climb. As a fledgling gymnast I immediately put two and two together and began carrying a block of magnesium carbonate with me when I visited the rocks. Climbers from both coasts and some Europeans saw me using it in the Tetons and the word spread, I suppose.

FLASH: Will you describe the process of doing efficient dynos? Did you train for these in the gym?

GILL: If you are a gymnast, dynamics are instinctive. I would practice occasionally on the women's uneven parallel bars, hanging in an L-position on the lower bar, then hopping to the upper bar with my hands only. The twenty-foot rope climb required a tremendous dynamic start from a seated L-position on the floor, with no boost from the legs. This helped on the rock.

On boulders I would pause in a hang or on a set of holds beneath an overhang, stare for a moment at the terminal handhold, then look down unfocused, and on a mental count of three pop up. Films show me looking again upward as I flew toward the handhold on top, but this never really registered consciously.

FLASH: Ironically, you also put up a few "no hands" boulder problems that many persons had difficulty ascending with their hands! What was the reason for the no-hands problems, a means of training footwork, or were they just for fun?

GILL: I wanted to cover a wide spectrum of bouldering and climbing difficulty, and the use of well-honed gymnastic balance appealed to me. I also wanted to test the limits of balance and footwork, isolated from a complete climbing experience. Once I did a simple fifth-class spire in Estes Park entirely no-hands. Royal descended Half Dome no-hands, I believe, so I wasn't alone in this peculiar pursuit. I was testing and pushing the frontiers of personal technique during this "Golden Age" of rock climbing. There were so many options then, and one could be at the leading edge with relatively modest preparation.

I don't think I would become a climber if I were a young man now – too much glitz and structure, too many peers, and the frontiers are well explored and very hard to approach. Too much of a social atmosphere, with its attendant pressures. What is freedom to a bird if it is in the middle of a flock?

FLASH: What other practices did you employ to help improve your footwork, balance, and technique?

GILL: I did a lot of slack-wire/chain walking, as did Pat Ament, my old friend and fellow gymnast. I don't believe this has much of a positive carry-over to climbing, for the balance is kinetic, not static. No-hands bouldering problems are excellent training for footwork.

FLASH: Have you ever climbed on any of the indoor walls in Colorado?

GILL: Never. I climbed briefly on the wall at Guisely, England, with the developer in 1986, but I haven't cared to visit other walls. The atmosphere is a bit too formal for me these days, also a little too social. I can draw magic out of the rock in solitude, but designer climbing walls are merely technical apparatus. When I was much younger, I would improvise – climb inside gymnasiums, and on buildings. It was more fun than climbing would have been on surfaces specifically designed for the climber.

FLASH: Finally, when it comes to balancing training and actual climbing time, what do you think are the ideal proportions?

GILL: In retrospect, if I had more opportunities to actually climb, rather than train, I might have gone a little bit further. I became a trifle too bulky with the special gymnastic abilities I developed. Ironically, I now weigh ten to twelve pounds less than I did 20 or 30 years ago, and the enhanced lightness compensates for the loss of muscular strength. I think, for bouldering particularly, the more time one spends on a variety of difficult rock problems, the better. On the other hand, training on simulated climbing moves or special apparatus can become an end in itself – much like a kata is to a martial artist. Thus unfolds the important aspect of climbing as ritual, pointing the way to unusual and pleasing experiences on the rock that are far removed from mainstream climbing.

FLASH: Unlike many activities, climbing requires the integration of mental and physical powers. In Master Of Rock, you describe two unique performance states – one in which you are "saturated in kinesthetic awareness," the other a "hypnagogic" state. Can you explain these states, when they occur, or how they emerge?

GILL: Kinesthetic awareness can be experienced when, in excellent form, one does a wired sequence over fairly difficult rock. Ask an accomplished gymnast or dancer about the feeling of flow, the almost rapturous sensation of dynamic lightness. Actually, the level of difficulty does not need to be high, although when it is, levels of enjoyment do seem to be greater. This has some connection with the finding of one's natural path in Taoism. This is the flow I seek as a middle-aged option-soloer.

The hypnagogic state – that twilight zone between sleep and consciousness – is associated with what Carlos Casteneda describes as the Art of Dreaming. Surprisingly, for a work of fiction, the procedures as detailed in his Don Juan books work quite efficiently to place one in fully conscious alternate reality. Ten or so years ago I did a fair amount of experimentation along these lines and was eventually able to "awaken" in a climbing environment and "climb" with a truly ecstatic feeling of lightness and freedom. The trick, then, is to merge this reality with the one in which we normally function. I was able to accomplish this feat on several occasions while climbing easy to moderate, well-rehearsed routes on nearby granite towers.

I can drift easily, even today, in that direction while climbing, but it takes a large measure of solitude. That is one reason why, during the warm summer months, I travel to isolated desert mountains, domes of golden granite where it is unlikely I will meet anyone. Difficulty by itself has become relatively immaterial, and climbs that are too serious restrict me from entering these zones. Option-soloing allows the right amount of potential variety to find and follow my path.

FLASH: In Master Of Rock you also mention a possible state of "telekinesis"!

GILL: The word "telekinesis" arose in an old interview when I had finished a bottle of wine, following a large spaghetti dinner! What I was getting at is the transcendent lightness an accomplished climber feels on occasion, and how easy it is to wonder if one really is that light. Is there psychic phenomena generated in the execution of some moves? Fun to speculate, but I suspect it's all in one's head.

FLASH: I believe that a positive mental state (even a smile) has the ability to energize, and that it may often be the determining factor in whether one succeeds or fails. What are your thoughts on this subject? Is "belief the Mother of reality"?

GILL: You are entirely correct. Also, "belief is the Mother of (alternate) realities."

FLASH: How far can belief and desire take a climber?

GILL: Into some rather unusual "zones," as well as being requirements for spectacular technical feats in normal reality, I suspect.

FLASH: I know you've commented that "vanity is a cardinal sin for climbers." What is the role of ego in climbing?

GILL: A strong, resilient ego is required for survival – and that's what we're talking about – on some desperate climbs. This muscular ego, which grows with success, can create a few problems from time to time in normal life, however!

FLASH: What is the best approach for attempting an unclimbed boulder or route?

GILL: Experimenting with various techniques with little regard to getting up the route the first try or being sensitive to the number of tries it takes. The latter has never been a concern of mine, although I have had friends who worship excessively at this altar. What is most important to me is doing the route well and smoothly – to milk the desperation out of the climb to as great a degree as possible. Also, have you ever noticed how an appallingly barren rock surface actually physically changes if you return to it two or three times? There must be alternate realities, parallel universes, in play here that I've never managed to control!

FLASH: Some climbers approach a route as if to go to war. Is this the most productive approach, or should a climber work with the rock? Is gravity a friend or foe?

GILL: I have never perceived myself as involved in a battle with nature. To find the patterns of flow is more my approach. This is a matter of tempering the ego. I have become blasphemously exercised from time to time, however, as my old bouldering companions will attest – so there is a non-trivial void between theory and practice! Try to maintain a sense of humor when climbing.

FLASH: How do you view the future of the sport? Is level of difficulty open-ended or are we approaching human limits? Will the greatest barriers in the future be mental or physical?

GILL: Which branch of the sport? Bouldering or Sport Climbing? Some other hybrids may emerge, too. It's up to the young to speculate and experiment. That's what I did 35 years ago. . .

I expect we've reached a gently rising plateau of difficulty, where harder individual moves will most frequently be facilitated by unusual anatomy. Seen in this way, the very concept of "difficult" undergoes subtle changes. Perhaps some new and novel twist on dynamics will be discovered. I used to speculate about a "double dynamic" sequence, where one uses the momentum of the first dynamic move to propel one's self into the beginning of a second dynamic move. I experimented on the rock, but the time wasn't ripe for such a bizarre accomplishment. The basics of dynamics had yet to be established.

Putting together longer and longer sequences in the area of Sport Climbing – both on constructed walls and natural rock – will present a continuing challenge, I suspect. When difficulty levels stabilize, risk is added to the formula. The psychological challenge will be just as great as the physical. On the other hand, new technical devices may appear that will be quickly adopted and will change the structure of the sport in an instant: fiberglass vaulting poles over bamboo; sticky rubber shoes; and perhaps a hand mitt comparable to modern sticky footgear will become available and become a standard accessory after a leading climber starts using it. Then the paradigm of the evolving sport changes. Read the classic *Games Climbers Play* by Tejada-Flores.

FLASH: What does the future hold for John Gill?

GILL: My underlying drive is a continuing and perhaps instinctive love of climbing – the euphoric feeling of controlled upward motion. I wax dangerously poetic when I contemplate this basic predisposition. When I was younger, I would climb anything. I still will. Recently I visited my elderly mother in Alabama and spent two sessions climbing up and down the 60-foot steel towers used by the football coaches at the University of Alabama. What younger climbers would be caught doing something so trivial? No challenge, merely vertical motion and a touch of exposure.

Beyond this primordial instinct, the second feature of the sport that motivates me to keep going is exploration. The urge to explore something new is satisfying in the modest mathematical research I do, as well as in my climbing. Perhaps this is another reason I don't care for artificial climbing walls.

Then comes the difficulty, the dynamics, the advanced technique, perhaps the risk and the commitment, etc. That's what motivates many climbers and what compelled me to do some of my harder routes. But, of course, I would have missed any number of ecstatic experiences had this been the sole focus of my climbing career.

LYNN HILL - THE CHAMP

Introduction by John Long

I first saw Lynn Hill at Trash Can Rock out at Joshua Tree, probably around 1976. Her brothers Bob and Jim were trying to teach her the ropes, though clearly she wore the harness in that family, having already taken the lead, fumbling with the carabiners and nuts and eventually giving up and waltzing up the 5.8 slab unprotected. Perhaps 16, she had a tight little gymnast's body, a face like a picture, and a shock of sandy hair under a wool Grand Prix driver's hat. Any fool could see she had a gift. Back then, when most female climbers were bored girlfriends, hippies, or peculiar in the extreme (I don't know why), it seemed strange and novel to see an athletic girl on the crags.

I can't remember seeing her for a couple of years until we were out at Josh again. John Bachar and I were standing below an obscure boulder, our fingertips shredded, arguing whether a certain problem was B1 or B2. Then "Little Lynny" (as we later styled her) showed up. She wasn't a girl anymore. She climbed the goddam boulder problem on her second try. "I guess it's only B1," I carped to Bachar. Hard to say, though, because I couldn't do it, then or ever.

No telling how it happened, but we fell in, and over the next four or five years, sort of grew up together. Of course, it only took another summer for Lynn to establish herself as one of the country's best climbers. But I was no less impressed – astonished, really – with her prowess in other sports. I remember my last year in grad school, when every night Lynn would drive up to Claremont where I worked in a racquetball club/weight-lifting gym. I spent much more time playing racquetball and working out than pushing the mop (my job), and because Lynn also loved to work out, we did so together. The boss, an ex-powerlifter, got Lynn on a program, and within six weeks she could routinely best the then-world-record bench press for her weight – something like 150 pounds, weighing 105 herself. Geez, was that girl strong! And fit.

Several years later she got recruited by the track coach at Santa Monica City College. With no running experience whatsoever, and after just a few months of training, Lynn placed third in the 1500 meters and fourth in the 3000 meters at the state meet, pushing SMC to championship. She also used to completely trash the competition, many of whom were Olympic athletes, at the annual Survival of the Fittest competition, a made-for-TV event consisting of grueling rope climbs, cross-country runs, and so forth. So you see, there's not so much mystery about why Lynn Hill is such a splendid climber. She simply came into this world with more natural gifts that the rest of us.

Of course we all know how Lynn went on to become a world champion sport climber, the one to beat, a mere five-foot girl who could climb as well as the very best men. But few people know all the adventure climbing she did early on – numerous trips up El Cap, hideous and dangerous free ascents in the Red Rocks, et al. There is about this career a majestic continuity. She always climbed like a champion, and even after she quits, she'll still carry herself like one and people will continue to call her one, so long as she lives – and long afterwards.

But what always impressed me more than the climbing and weights and running and stuff I've since forgotten, is what a terrific and rare human being she is. She never has a bad word for anyone, and seems to think that when life hurls problems at her, they are always her doing, which is rarely

Champ Lynn Hill at Snowbird, 1992.

Chris Goplerud photo

the case. She's the most natively kind and guileless person I've ever met, and though success and failure and sponsors have tempered her a bit, I doubt there is anything she wouldn't do for a friend.

About the time I started tromping through jungles around the South Pacific, Lynn and I drifted apart. Now she lives in France, and I spend much of the year in Venezuela, and it's rare that we're both in town at the same time. But we always get together when we are, and we remain close friends. I got her into a sea kayak some months ago, then refused to take her again. She had a natural stroke and fine balance and damn if I'm going to have her whip me at my own sport – again.

FLASH: You have been climbing for nearly two decades and for much of that time you've been climbing at the cutting edge of difficulty. To what do you attribute such consistency and longevity?

HILL: I believe it's mostly mental. Being able to stay energized day to day and year to year is a challenge. I've always been a curious kind of person. This curiosity to learn is a large part of what keeps me going.

FLASH: Can you be more specific about the mental aspects of climbing, as you see it?

HILL: Relaxation, acceptance, and keeping an open mind are key. First of all, peak performance isn't possible if one is not relaxed, and if one is going to stay relaxed they must simply accept problems when they arise and decide to solve them. If I can't do a move I merely accept that I haven't discovered the right sequence, instead of trying the same sequence over and over or just quitting. I will try to do it 20 or 30 different ways, making subtle changes in body position and foot placement, until I find something that does work. That's what I mean by keeping an open mind.

FLASH: So if you can't initially do a move, you don't just put it off as a reach problem or lack of strength?

HILL: No. Reach and strength are rarely the limiting factors. Many times strength is just a matter of concentration – so it goes back to mental things again! I just try to keep an open mind and use creativity and positive visualization to meet the challenge and hopefully solve the problem.

FLASH: What do you consider to have been your biggest accomplishments? Is there a point in time you felt like you broke some kind of barrier?

HILL: I don't like the word "barrier" because it implies limits. However, I have made it past a few "caps" in performance – I guess you could say breakthroughs. For one, my on-sight of a route called Simone (10-) in Germany was significant because it represented the first 5.13b on-sight by a woman.

Another big ascent for me was Mass Critique (8b) in France. It was the first redpoint of a 5.14a by a woman. Also, the circumstances of the ascent made it even more special. I worked the route for several days after which I truly felt like I could do it. But I had an injured finger and only three days left in France before having to fly back to the States. So I rested for two of the days to recover fully and then went back and did it first try on my last day in the country!

Most recently, my first free ascent of the Nose on El Cap was really special because it was in the aftermath of my competition career, and it kind of tied all I've done in the past together.

FLASH: During your long climbing career you've done so many different types of climbing. Certainly this has helped elevate your technical skills to rare levels. What moves have you found most important or crucial to success at the high numbers?

HILL: High stepping, adjusting my body positions for maximum proficiency, using lots of intermediate holds, drooping myself in power positions like before exploding in a dynamic thrust or lunging (I do a lot of lunging), and turning to the side (hip turns and drop-knees) to gain maximum reach. I should point out that concentration is critical for precise execution of most, if not all, of these. For instance, when doing lunges you must hit it just right and be very confident that you'll stick it. Belief is key because if there's any thought that you might be too small or something, you probably won't get it.

FLASH: I guess that's true of any move or for any person.

HILL: Oh yeah. So often I find myself using unchalked intermediate holds to get by improbable reaches or lunges. They might be too small to use for advancement, hence no chalk on them, but I look for anything that I can use to better set up a move. Even the most unlikely holds can be used to improve balance or body position and to guide trajectories when lunging.

FLASH: Now on to strength training...Do you think sport-specific training for climbing is overrated?

HILL In a sense. Some people place too much importance on strength training. Too many people think it is the way to get better, when in reality there are so many other things to consider such as technique, mental control, flexibility, and many others. Sure everybody can use more strength, but isolating your training to just strength is definitely not good.

FLASH: Do you do regular sport-specific strength training?

HILL: Not really. I supplement my climbing with complementary things like running, stretching, some gymnastic exercises, and such, but mostly during the off-season. General exercises like these help overall conditioning and help prevent muscle-imbalance injures.

FLASH: So I guess climbing on rock and plastic provide your "specific" training to the fingers, arms, and such?

HILL: Yes. I prefer rock – climbing at many different cliffs. But when the weather is bad I'll train on plastic at friends' houses. Many climbers here in France have home walls, especially the leading climbers who spend most of their time on them. So it's easy to call someone and go train with them.

FLASH: What's your focus when training on plastic?

HILL: On plastic, you can invent different problems that require specific techniques or power moves. Actually, I probably don't do this enough. This year I plan to do more of that because for me what I lack most is power. I have a lot of natural endurance, so I think I could make some gains in power if I bouldered more on these home walls.

Also, I occasionally isolate things like one- or two-finger strength. I train this with the help of bungee cords or latex tubes and little by little find the right amount of "help" so I can do a one-arm hang, two-finger pull-up, or whatever.

FLASH: What are your fundamental beliefs when it comes to training?

HILL: I think the most important things are having friends to train with, training quality over quantity, having goals, finding a proper balance between training and climbing, depending on your goals and the time you have available, and training according to your genetic potential. If you have a natural tendency toward more power you should probably work endurance, etc.

FLASH: How about rest days? Do you plan your schedule out days in advance?

HILL: At home I generally stick to a two days on, one day off schedule. Depending on how I feel or what I'm climbing I might rest a bit more or climb more. However, if I climb more than two days in a row it's usually because I'm not climbing at a super-high level, I'm climbing easy routes.

FLASH: How about your diet?

HILL: I'm very conscientious about what I eat and how much. I like fresh, natural foods that aren't refined. I try to cook most of my food because then I can control exactly what I'm getting. Of course, I avoid empty calories like sugars and alcohol. Pretty much common sense stuff...but quite important if you want to be lean.

FLASH: Have you noticed a difference in how Europeans approach climbing verses their American counterparts?

HILL: I've been living in France about three years now and the basic difference I've noticed is that people climb more often, maybe because there's a higher concentration of rock and the weather is generally better, especially in the south. And of course, there's a higher concentration of hard routes and good climbers to train with. You are constantly surrounded by people who are examples of good technique and motivation.

Of course there are also cultural differences that affect the ways things are. People here don't make a big deal about on-sighting hard routes or redpointing 5.13. There are so many good climbers here and they aren't all out looking for sponsors or even asking for free shoes. They are a bit more humble, and I guess more people here climb just for the sake of doing it. For most, it's something they've been doing since they were kids.

FLASH: What does the future hold for Lynn Hill?

HILL: The main thing is to do more enjoyable climbs! I have some projects I want to finish, in particular a book I've been working on. Also, I'm designing a line of holds for Entre Prise that will be available later this year.

I plan to travel to some new places like Nepal and Tibet, maybe Africa. I like to climb in beautiful places, but I won't do anything too desperate!

And I plan to do a film...I want to do the Nose free in a day! It's in the planning stages now and will hopefully come to fruition later this year.

MIA AXON – GRACE UNDER PRESSURE

Mia Axon has been climbing since she was a teenager but has just now come into her own at the age of 34. Formerly a professional harpist, she now works nine-to-five as a fund-raiser, trains two or three evenings during the work week, and climbs on weekends.

Mia had a sensational year in 1993. Not only has she redpointed 5.13 at the crags but she has risen quickly to become one of the best female competition climbers in America. Earlier this year she won the Nationals at Paradise in Denver and more recently the Nationals at Hunter Mountain, New York. Mia is living proof that people with full-time jobs can be great climbers!

In this interview Mia tells us how she became one of the most consistent competition climbers around. Whether you're an ASCF competitor or just planning to compete at your local gym this winter, I'm sure you'll gain some valuable insight into mental and physical preparations for competitions.

FLASH: Your competition record this year is as good as any with a win at the Tour De Pump series and two national competitions. To what do you attribute your consistency in either winning or placing near the top in every comp you enter?

AXON: My new job has regular hours around which I can structure a solid training and climbing schedule. This consistency in my training is what I think made the difference. I'm able to work hard on the physical end as well as improve on the mental aspects.

FLASH: *Competitions are certainly very mental. How do you train for dealing with the pressures of competition?*

AXON: There's no good way other than to compete a lot. A person's level of success in anything is often a direct reflection

Mia Axon on her way to winning the 1993 Nationals at Hunter Mountain, New York.

Michael Kodus photo

of how much time he or she puts into that endeavor. I think the local comps like the Tour de Pump here on the Front Range are an exceptional opportunity for people to get used to what competition climbing is all about. The more you're exposed to the pressure, the better you become at dealing with it.

FLASH: Do you think previous competition experience in other sports translates at all to climbing competitions?

AXON: Absolutely. I was both a gymnast and a professional harpist. You can apply a certain amount of that kind of experience.

FLASH: On-sight climbing is a major part of competition climbing. Does on-sighting a lot on rock translate to on-sight success on plastic?

AXON: I think on-sight practice on rock is wonderful. But from a time perspective you can often get in more climbing at a gym. This is especially important for people with full-time jobs. Practicing in gyms has really helped me out.

FLASH: Any tricks or techniques you apply in the gym to make on-sighting harder, or to make for better practice?

AXON: Sometimes I attempt on-sights without previewing the route. This teaches you to on-sight while you climb. In comps you can often figure the bottom part during the preview period, but you can't see the holds so well 30 feet up the route. This technique helps prepare you for that.

FLASH: What's your ratio of days climbing on rock to days training in the gym?

AXON: For most of the year it's even. My workouts during the week are generally on plastic; on weekends I get out on real rock. Of course, during the winter most of the time I'm climbing inside.

FLASH: When you're in the gym, are you usually leading or do you boulder and TR a lot?

AXON: I always try to have a plan when I walk through the door. I just don't go in and climb. Ultimately, it depends on whether my goal for that workout is to train for endurance, power, or on-sighting. The plan is somewhat flexible, though, depending on my energy levels or who I am working out with.

FLASH: Do you prefer to train with people at your level?

AXON: I like to have a lot of variety in who I train with. I enjoy climbing with people who have a lot of energy, even if they are climbing 5.9s. In this case, I might have a little lighter-than-usual workout. However, if I'm working hard stuff, I like to have someone of that caliber to work with. It's kind of a sharing thing. You can learn from each other. That's a good reason to climb with a wide range of people.

FLASH: Take us through a typical climbing gym workout!

AXON: The typical session is three hours. Of course, I start with some warm-ups and stretching, then do some traversing. What I do for the main part of my workout depends on where I am. Once a week I go to CATS (Colorado Athletic Training School) and work power. The harness will never go on because my focus is hard boulder problems. The next workout I might be at Paradise Rock Gym, which has some nice lead walls, so I'll work more on endurance and leading.

FLASH: What about specific strength-training exercises?

AXON: I always save them for the end of the workout...to finish myself off. Paradise has a Campus Board I like working, and CATS has some gymnastic equipment, which is really conducive to working pull-up and lock-off type exercises.

FLASH: What mental attitude do you take into a comp? What do you think about on the day before or the morning of the comp?

AXON: For me it's really important that I relax the day before. I get plenty of training time in during the week, but with work I don't always get the rest I should. If I can get the day before off, that's the best. I do some stretching and prepare things such as cleaning my shoes.

I sometimes get jitters before comps. Fortunately, I've been consistent, so I can remind myself of that and remain confident. That's always a good trick to use when you get nervous before a climb. Think about and visualize past performances that went well. This gives confidence and should help relieve some of the jitters.

FLASH: What advice can you give FLASH readers about strategy on the day of the comp? To start with, what do you look for during the five minute preview?

AXON: The first thing you do is scan the route so you know the general direction the climb takes. Then you try to figure out the sequence from bottom to top. If you have time, it's also good to work the moves backwards from the top down. This is especially helpful in solving confusing sections where you're unsure about which hands should be on what holds.

Then look for holds that might be hidden, like around a corner. Try to identify where the cruxes and rests are. Look for stem rests, heel hooks, knee bars, etc. It's also important to determine the exact hold from which you will make each clip – this is critical!

Finally, look at the route as a whole and determine the best general strategy. Does the route appear to have lots of rests? If so you may be able to take your time and climb more slowly. Or is the route steep, with no obvious rest? In this case, your best strategy would be to just keep moving and beat the pump.

FLASH: What should you NOT be thinking about or doing?

AXON: If you can't figure out a section, then skip it and look through the rest of the route. Interaction with the other competitors can be helpful and in my opinion is very positive. Shared information can help some. If you're not sure about a particular hold, ask someone if they know it! Again, most people are positive in this area although I'm not sure if these exchanges ultimately affect the results much. In the long run the best climber usually comes out on top.

FLASH: After the preview it's common to spend hours in isolation. How do you occupy your time?

AXON: Isolation is interesting. It can be quite social because most of the people are your friends. Some people talk a lot and have fun; however, I'm a bit more serious. I prefer to be off by myself visualizing the route and listening to my walkman some. Of course, I do spend some time on the warm-up wall, but a good 20- or 30-minute rest is necessary before I head out to climb.

FLASH: When you get out to the wall to climb, what are you thinking?

AXON: First, I always visualize myself getting to the top! Next I might check out part of the route again if I was having trouble visualizing – remembering it back in isolation.

FLASH: Are you really able to remember the whole route?

AXON: That's something I'm working on. I'm getting better! It's an acquired skill you must practice regularly. Something else I'd like to stress to FLASH readers is that competition climbing isn't just climbing. It's also a lot of rules. It's easy to get so focused that you make a dumb mistake. Before you start climbing, quickly review the out-of-bounds markers and the rules relating to stepping off the ground. That one caught me once.

FLASH: And once you begin climbing?

AXON: Be confident and decisive. And flash!

FLASH: On another subject, I know you wanted to mention a few words about the American Mountain Foundation (AMF)?

AXON: Yes, the AMF is a climbing-oriented, non-profit organization that helps to mitigate the impact climbers have. They do things like trail building, as well as work with public land managers to help keep climbing areas accessible. They are similar to the Access Fund but with a bit more of an environmental slant.

FLASH: How can climbers get involved?

AXON: They can certainly make a donation to the AMF and lend their hands to work projects. Most importantly, they can have good stewardship over the places they climb!

FLASH: You have a long and uniquely diverse climbing career ranging from run-out traditional routes to extreme sport routes. Can you give us a brief history of your career?

SMITH: Right out of high school (1982) I moved to Joshua Tree for the winter season, then eventually to Yosemite. I was drawn by the experiences to be had – the exposure, adrenaline, and I wanted to climb as much as possible. I was adventurous and wanted to do it all: bouldering, big walls, long free cracks, run-out faces, ice climbing, you name it. There was this big scene, and the main focus was to have fun and climb a lot. It wasn't too competitive, and big numbers certainly weren't that important – style was everything!

FLASH: How long did you remain in that scene? When did you discover sport climbing?

SMITH: It was the summer of '88 when I first wanted to try sport climbing. That was the year of the first Snowbird comp, and I was psyched to attend and compete. It was another experience to try. Unfortunately, I wrecked my knee skateboarding a week before the comp. That injury laid me up for a while, and I had a lot of time to think. Ultimately my whole perspective changed. I decided I wanted to continue climbing for a long time but not have to worry about getting injured. Of course, my ground-up style of doing hard, often dangerous, traditional routes was in conflict with that desire...I was definitely on a path that could have led to an even more severe injury.

I became captivated with the idea of pushing my physical limits. Up to that point, climbing was often about pushing the mental limits. I guess I realized I wanted to do harder rock climbs yet never have to get injured again.

FLASH: So it did become a bit of a "numbers" thing?

SMITH: It was more about what I could personally envision and then do. For me the focus has always been first ascents – seeing a blank piece of rock, first conceiving then believing in the line, and finally making it reality. Sport climbing allowed me to open my eyes and discover what I could do in terms of pushing my physical limits.

FLASH: It sounds like you felt you had pushed the traditional limits as far as they could go without a greater risk of getting hurt or killed.

SMITH: Definitely. I had pushed deep into the 5.12 grade on routes that were really run out. In fact when the first sport climbers said "you can't put up 5.13's without rap-bolting," I had already put up a few 5.13a's ground-up, no hang dogging, pulling the rope, etc. And those routes were real sporty. You could definitely get messed up if you blew it.

Kurt Smith, one of the hardest training climbers around, pumpin some 'way steep' limestone at Rifle, Colorado.

Chris Goplerud photo

FLASH: After your injury where was the first area you went to experience sport climbing?

SMITH: Shelf Road. Getting on that pocketed limestone the first time was a really neat experience! I was still wearing a knee brace, and the safety of the bolted routes was nice. After having pushed the mental aspect of the sport for so long, it was so great to be able to concentrate on movement and gymnastic difficulty.

FLASH: Back to the early days. Who were your mentors?

SMITH: John Bachar, Michael Lechlinski, John Yablonski, and Ron Kauk. I climbed a lot with those guys, and in hindsight I was really lucky to have such a rich environment in which I could really grow. A beginner can watch a really good climber and model what they're doing. My technique improved quickly by going bouldering or doing routes with those guys, and observing, visualizing, and executing moves in a similar way.

FLASH: What kind of sport-specific training did they expose you to?

SMITH: Bachar had this whole gym set up with ladders, wooden fingerboards, overhanging climbing (Death) boards, pull-up rigs with weights and counter-weights, dip bars, and a bar to do some gymnastics exercises like some of Gill's stuff.

FLASH: Do you think those kind of workouts really helped, or did they focus too much on power?

SMITH: Everybody needs more power! But in the long run you'll definitely be held back if you don't work on all the other things that affect performance.

FLASH: How do your current workouts differ from those in the early days?

SMITH: Everything is much more regimented, and I'm certainly more religious about it. I train a ton and everything has to be cycled just right so I don't have too many, or too few, rest days. The goal is maximum gains without getting injured and that's a matter of listening to your body and learning how it reacts to various workouts.

A big thing is avoiding boredom. I vary my workouts a lot between training at the crags, in the gym, and a combination of bouldering and plastic (artificial holds) workouts in the same day. If I'm at Rifle, I'll do a bunch of warm-up routes, then work on my project, and then just trash myself on hard routes that I have wired.

FLASH: How many warm-up routes is a "bunch"?

SMITH: Five or six, maybe more...Normally I'd start by doing a few 11's then stretch and recover for a while. Next I'd run up a few 12's, maybe a 13a that I have really wired and work on getting a deep pump so the muscles are warmed throughout. I'd then stretch some more and take a long rest before I move on to the project.

FLASH: But if your project is to redpoint something ridiculously hard, then you still need to be 100 percent fresh when you get on it! Most people wouldn't think of doing that many warm-up climbs before a big redpoint attempt.

SMITH: Many people don't warm-up enough. Plus there's more to warming-up for a big redpoint than just getting the muscles ready. You must work out all the mental jitters, pretense, and apprehension, so that you are really ready for business!

FLASH: Slice Of Life (14a) is your hardest route to date. Was completing it a matter of breaking physical barriers or was it more of a mental thing – getting yourself to believe in it?

SMITH: For sure, it was a physical barrier because I never put a route together that was that long and continuously hard, and with no "camping." I first had to train on the bottom part so I could climb it fast and without wasting too much energy. I needed to arrive at the crux fresh. Then once I could do that, it still took me a while to stick the crux lunge – that may have been a mental problem more than anything. It was a matter of getting myself to relax and just do the move as if I were bouldering off the ground. Once I stuck the lunge, I had always thought I'd float to the top! But instead I had to fight up the final 30 feet, which is still 13a. I became so pumped that it turned into a full-on mental battle to hang on and get to the top. I kept telling myself "just one more move, just one more move..." all the way up that last 30 feet!

FLASH: Sounds like it turned into a brawl?

SMITH: It may have ended up being one of the most un-beautiful, unpleasant redpoints of my life, but it was also the greatest feeling of accomplishment. I was so pumped towards the end – I should have been sent all over the place – but mentally I was strong enough to finish the route. At one point I was pulling the rope to clip and my other hand started to open on the hold, so I dropped the rope, skipped the clip, and kept on climbing.

FLASH: When you finally did Slice, you had put in over 60 redpoint tries in four months of work. How did you keep your motivation up for so long?

SMITH: It was hard for me to do that, but I kept telling myself that this was the culmination of 15 years of climbing. Over 350 first ascents had led up to this one route, this one vision. So the longer it took me to do the route the more it meant to me. The number grade is really irrelevant. It could be downgraded tomorrow, and I really wouldn't care. What I care about is that I didn't give up. Day after day the route would kick my ass. I'd keep fighting it and it would keep sending me. But I stayed focused and eventually sent it!

FLASH: Are you worried about it getting downgraded? Deserved or not, it's kind of a game some people like to play.

SMITH: Several excellent climbers have been on the route, but no one's done it yet. One individual thought it might be 13d, but you can't really say until you do it. The French team is coming in this year, so I'm sure Francois Legrand or someone will send it – killer! The bottom line is that there are a few climbers who have to come down off their ego and their little high horse, and realize that Americans are training harder and getting better. It's not true that everything in America is overgraded. Some areas like Rifle, when compared to Europe, are right on the money. The problem is that there are too many climbers that get off on bashing other people.

FLASH: It may be that such a negative approach may hurt American climbing more than the overgrading of some routes?

SMITH: There's always going to be some bitching – every sport has it, but it's getting out of control, and the magazines only seem to hype it more.

FLASH: You now have a new project near Slice that looks even harder? What are your workouts like?

SMITH: When I'm not at the crags and training at home, I like to get two or three sessions per day. I'll usually start out in the morning with some stretching at home, then go to one of the nearby bouldering areas like Morrison and warm-up on some problems with good holds. When ready I begin on problems that emphasize powerful movements, then as I tire I work into longer link-ups that are less difficult.

This session may last for a couple hours, then I rest for two hours and head to one of the gyms. Here I may boulder some more, but the main focus is on leading. I think it's important to practice on-sight climbing regularly, and a gym that changes its routes frequently is a good place to "hang." After I do some on-sighting, I'll work on something really hard. Once I'm blown, I'll pack it up and head for home. Again, I rest for about two hours then finish off in my attic, which is a good place to build a steep home gym! Similar to the first session, I begin with short powerful problems and end with longer endurance traverses that contain frequent crux moves that make you dig deep into the power reserves!

FLASH: Unfortunately, most climbers lack the facilities and time to execute such a routine!

SMITH: They must remember that everyone is different and that it's all relative to your ability and goals. But the basics are the same: you must train on rock or plastic regularly, and it's best to train power before endurance.

FLASH: What other training exercises do you perform?

SMITH: I cycle in a fingerboard workout on occasion. I like the bigger holds that slope because they're easy on the fingers but hard to hang on. I avoid any painful holds that might injure me like small crimps or shallow monodoights (one-finger pockets). Also, I like to do fingerboard or campus board workouts alone. If the workout becomes competitive or the ego games begin, you can end up getting hurt. It's not worth getting injured.

FLASH: What's your workout/climbing schedule like?

SMITH: I prefer two days on, one off, two on, one off, two on, two off. But I also frequently do two on, one off, two on, two off. Obviously, this isn't a schedule a beginner should adopt, but after 15 years of climbing I'm able to stretch it out a bit.

FLASH: Do you ever deviate from this routine?

SMITH: I do, if my body tells me to!

FLASH: I understand you are getting into climbing-gym design. What are your favorite gyms to date?

SMITH: The gym I designed in Dallas is, of course, quite nice! It's called Exposure and is the first climbing gym in Texas. Also, Solid Rock in San Diego (designed by Mike Pont) and Rockreation in Salt Lake City (by Christian Griffith) are really good. My home gym also ranks up there!

FLASH: How about sponsors? Who is included in your support team?

SMITH: My wife Annie tops the list – also, La Sportiva, Petzl, Cousin Ropes, PowerBar, Bison Ball, Gregory packs, Exposure Rock Gym, and my Mom!

FLASH: What advice do you have for young, enthusiastic climbers, or for that matter any climber out there who wants to climb better?

SMITH: Get out and climb as many different types of routes, at as many different areas as possible. Many climbers are held back because they do the same routes at the same area, and they don't log a lot of different experiences and techniques. Experiment with training and find out what works best for you. And most importantly, have a positive attitude no matter what. Negative energy will send you down! Get focused on your goals and go after them, and forget about what the other guys are doing or saying – distractions like that will ultimately hold you back.

Kurt Smith hitting the crux lunge on "Slice of Life" (5.14a), Rifle, Colorado.

Chris Goplerud photo

Fitness Evaluation and Questionnaire

This fitness evaluation will serve as a tool with which you can periodically gauge your improvement in the physical aspects of climbing performance. What's more, a statistical study of the results will hopefully allow us at *Flash Training* to identify specific correlations relating to fitness, skill and overall climbing ability, among other things.

Please return your test results and questionnaire (a copy of these pages will do fine) to us. In return, we will be glad to ship you a free "JUST SEND IT" / *Flash Training* bumper sticker, but please send a self-addressed, stamped envelope.

Fitness Evaluation

To ensure accurate results it is best to perform the test exercises when you are completely fresh (i.e. after at least two days rest). Since many of the exercises are extremely strenuous, it is ideal to break up the testing over a couple of workouts and, by all means, perform a comprehensive warm-up before performing these exercises.

Test 1: One-set maximum number of pull-ups. Do this test on a standard pull-up bar with your palms away and hands shoulder-width apart. Do not bounce and be sure to go up and down the whole way.

Evaluation: Total number of pull-ups in a single go.

Results:_____

Test 2: One-repetition maximum pull-up. Do a single pull-up with a 10 pound weight clipped to your harness. Rest two minutes, then add 10 more pounds and repeat.

Evaluation: The maximum amount of added weight successfully lifted for a single pull-up divided by your body weight.

Results:_____

Test 3: One-arm lock-off (described in Chapter 2). Start with a standard chin-up (palms facing) then lock-off at the top on one arm and let go with the other.

Evaluation: Length of time in the lock-off before your chin drops below the bar.

Results: Right arm_____ Left arm _____

Test 4: One-set maximum number of Frenchies. Perform the exercise as described in Chapter 2. Remember, each cycle consists of three pull-ups separated by the three different lock-off positions which are held for seven seconds. Have a partner time your lock-offs.

Evaluation: The number of cycles (or part of) completed in a single set.

Results: _____

Test 5: One-set maximum number of fingertip pull-ups on a three-fourths inch _____ edge (approximately 1.5cm). Perform this exercise as in Test 1 except on a fingerboard edge or doorjamb of approximately the stated size.

Evaluation: The number of fingertip pull-ups done in a single go.

Results:_____

Test 6: Lock-off in the top position of a fingertip pull-up (three-fourths inch edge) for as long as possible.

Evaluation: Length of time in the lock-off until your chin drops below the edge.

Results: _____

Test 7: Straight-arm hang from a standard pull-up bar as described in Chapter 2.

Evaluation: Length of time you can hang on the bar before muscle failure.

Results:_____

Test 8: One-set maximum number of sit-ups. Perform these on a pad or carpeted floor with your knees bent at approximately 90 degrees, your feet flat on the floor and with nothing anchoring them. Also, do them with thumbs on your collar bone and elbows out to the side.

Evaluation: Number of sit-ups you can perform without stopping. Do them slowly and in control with no bouncing.

Results:_____

Test 9: Wall split as described in "Stretching for Climbing" in Chapter 2. Be sure your butt is no more than six inches from the wall.

Evaluation: Position your legs so they are equidistant from the floor and measure the distance from your heels to the floor.

Results: _____

Test 10: High-step as described in Chapter 2. Stand facing a wall with one foot flat on the floor with toes touching the wall. Lift the other leg up to the side as high as possible without any aid from the hands.

Evaluation: Measure the height of your step off the floor and divide it by your height.

Results:_____

QUESTIONNAIRE

1. Name _____

Address_____

City/State/Zip _____

2. Age_____ Sex_____

3. Height_____ Weight_____ Percent body fat if known _____

4. Previous sports background_____

5. Number of years climbing _____

6. Preferred type of climbing (sport, trad, bouldering, big wall) _____

7. Current on-sight lead ability (75% success rate) at what level _____

8. Hardest redpoint (worked route) _____

9. Are you currently doing sport-specific training for climbing? _____

10. Have you ever climbed on an indoor wall? _____

11. How often do you climb indoors (days per month)_____

12. Do you belong to a climbing gym? _____ Which ?_____

13. Have you ever participated in a climbing competition

_____

14. Have you ever been injured while climbing or training for climbing?____

If so, describe _____

15. Approximately how many days per year do you climb? ___

16. How many different climbing areas have you visited in the past 12 months? _____

17. What are your goals in this sport?

_____

18. What do you like best about *Flash Training*?

_____

19. What other subjects would you like to see addressed in future issues?

_____

20. Is there any particular expert climber you'd like to hear from or ask a question of?

_____

Please send a copy of your Fitness Evaluation and Questionnaire to the address below, as soon as possible. Include a self-addressed stamped envelope and we will promptly send you free-of-charge the "JUST SEND IT"/*Flash Training* sticker. Extra stickers are available for $2.00 each. Thank you!

Flash Training
Peak Performance America
P.O. Box 8633
Lancaster, PA 17604

Glossary

The following is a compilation of some of the technical terms and jargon used throughout this book. This is a strictly American glossary; the British, French, or Germans undoubtedly use somewhat different terminology.

acute: having rapid onset, severe symptoms and a short course; not chronic

aerobics: any physical activity deriving energy from the breakdown of glycogen in the presence of oxygen, thus producing little or no lactic acid, enabling an athlete to continue exercise much longer

aggro: short for aggressive

anorexia: pathological absence of appetite or hunger in spite of a need for food

Ape-index: fingertip to fingertip distance (across your chest with arms out to each side) minus your height; a positive Ape-index is associated with above-average reach for a given height

anaerobic: energy production in the muscles involving the breakdown of glycogen in the absence of oxygen. A by-product called lactic acid is formed resulting in rapid fatigue and cessation of physical activity

arousal: an internal state of alertness or excitement

ATP: a high-energy compound which is stored in the muscles in very small amounts. The body's ultimate fuel source

autonomous stage: an advanced stage of motor learning in which the learner develops automaticity in action and information processing

back-stepping: outside edging on a foothold which is behind you while climbing a move with your side to the wall

barndoor: sideways swinging or uncontrolled turning of the body resulting from poor balance or body positioning

batwing: extension of the wrist to increase leverage or grip of a hold which results in the elbow lifting away from the rock

beta: any prior information about a route including sequence, rests, gear, clips, etc.

bi-doigt: French for two-finger pocket

blocked practice: a practice sequence in which a specific task is practiced repeatedly

bouldering: variable practice of climbing skills performed without a belay rope at the base of a cliff or on small boulders

buildering: bouldering on man-made structures

camping: long, usually comfortable rests taken partway up a climb

campus board: a short version of the Death Board used specifically for training power

campusing: climbing an overhanging section of rock or artificial wall with no feet, usually in a dynamic left hand, right hand, left hand repeating sequence

capability: the internal representation of skill, acquired during practice, that allows performance of some task

chronic: long-term disorder; not acute

cognitive stage: the first stage of learning in which the primary determinants of success are related to decision making and intellectual functioning

contact strength: initial grip strength on a rock hold

crank: to pull down hard

crimp grip: the most natural and stressful way to grip a rock hold characterized by hyperextension of the first joint in the fingers and nearly full contraction of the second joint

crux: the hardest move, or sequence of moves, on a route

deadpoint: the "high" position of a dynamic move where, for a moment, all motion stops

Death board: a training device consisting of horizontal strips of wood mounted on a long plank in a ladder-like configuration

detox: to shakeout, rest, and recover from a pump

dog: short for hangdog

drop-knee: an exaggerated back-step where one knee is dropped toward the ground while the other is pointing up, resulting in a stable chimney-like positioning of the legs, especially on overhanging rock

dynamic move: an explosive leap for a hold otherwise out of reach

dyno: short for dynamic

enzyme: protein produced by living tissue to accelerate metabolic reactions

epicondylitis: inflammation of the tendon origins of the forearm flexors (medial) or extensors (lateral) near the elbow

ergogenic: performance enhancing

flagging: a climbing technique in which one foot is crossed behind the other in order to avoid barndooring and to improve balance

flash: to climb a route on the first try without ever having touched the route, but with the aid of beta

flash pump: a rapid, often vicious, muscular pump resulting from strenuous training or climbing without first performing a proper, gradual warm-up

G-tox: a technique which uses gravity to help speed recovery from a forearm pump; it involves alternating the position of the resting arm between the normal "hanging-at-your-side" position and a "raised-hand" position above your shoulder

glycogen: compound chains of glucose stored in the muscle and liver for use during aerobic or anaerobic exercise glycemic index: a scale which classifies how the ingestion of various foods affects blood-sugar levels in comparison to the ingestion of straight glucose

gripped: extremely scared

hangdogging: "climbing" a route, usually bolt to bolt, with the aid of the rope to hang and rest

heel hook: use of the heel on a hold, usually above chest level, to aid in pulling and balance

honed: in extremely good shape, probably very ripped

hyperemia: an excess supply of blood and oxygen in a muscle which results from deep sportsmassage

hypertrophy: enlargement in size (e.g. muscular hypertrophy)

insulin: a hormone that decreases the blood glucose level

isometric: muscular contraction resulting in no shortening of the muscle (no movement)

kinesthetic: the sense derived from muscular contractions and limb movements

killer: extraordinarily good

lactic acid: acid by-product of the anaerobic metabolism of glucose during intense muscular exercise

ligament: collagenous connective tissue that attaches articular extremities of bones

lipids: broad term for fat and fat-like substances

lunge: an out of control dynamic move; a jump for a far off hold

manky: of poor quality, as in a manky finger jam or a manky protection placement

mental practice: practice in which the learner visualizes successful execution without overt physical practice

modeling: a learning technique where an individual watches, then attempts a skill as performed properly by another person

monodoigt: French for one-finger pocket

motor learning: a set of internal processes associated with practice or experience leading to a relatively permanent gain in performance capability

motor skill: a skill where the primary determinant of success is the movement component itself

motor stage: the second stage of learning, in which motor programs are developed and the performance becomes increasingly consistent

motor unit: a motor neuron, together with a group of muscle cells it stimulates, in an all or nothing response

on-sight: when a route is climbed first try and with absolutely no prior information of any kind

open-hand grip: the safer and more powerful grip involving only slight flexion of the first two joints of the fingers

option-soloing: solo climbing on "easy" terrain where many potential lines exist, with frequent easy scrambling alternatives, and many branch points allow for spontaneous decisions appropriate to a given moment

periodization: division of an annual plan into three phases of training – preparatory, competitive, and transition – to ensure peaking for the main competition(s) of the year

pH: the symbol commonly used to express hydrogen ion concentration in a solution, that is, to describe the degree of acidity or alkalinity

protein efficiency ratio (PER): gain in body weight per gram of protein consumed

psyched: raring to go or very happy

pumped: when the muscles become gorged with blood due to extended physical exertion

random practice: a practice sequence in which tasks from several classes are experienced in random order over consecutive trails

Recommended Dietary Allowances (RDA): quantities of specific vitamins, minerals, and protein needed daily that have been judged adequate for maintenance of good nutrition in the United States population, developed by the Food and Nutrition Board of the National Academy of Science

redpoint: lead climbing a route bottom to top in one push

reflexes: involuntary, rapid responses to stimuli

ripped: extreme muscular detail due to low body fat

schema: a set of rules, usually developed and applied unconsciously by the motor system in the brain and spinal cord, relating how to move and adjust muscle forces, body positions, etc., given the parameters at hand, such as steepness of the rock, friction qualities, holds being used, and type of terrain

send it!: an emphatic statement to someone encouraging them to hang in and finish a route without falling

sharp end: the lead climber's end of the rope

shred: to do really well, or to dominate

skill: a capability to bring about an end result with maximum certainty, minimum energy, and minimum time

sport climbing: usually refers to any indoor or outdoor

climbing on bolt-protected routes

sport psychology: the field of study relating to the application of psychological principles to sport performance

spotter: a person designated to slow the fall of a boulderer, with the main goal of keeping the boulderer's head from hitting the ground

stick-clip: use of a stick to clip an out-of-reach bolt, usually the first on a route

super recruiting: extreme, and potentially dangerous, power training utilizing "falling loads," which the muscles can not lift but can "catch"

tendinitis/tendonosis: a disorder involving the inflammation of a tendon and synovial membrane at a joint

tendon: a white fibrous cord of dense, regular connective tissue that attaches muscle to bone

trad: short for traditional climber – someone who prefers routes with natural protection, instead of bolts

training effect: a basic principle of exercise science which states that adaptation occurs from an exercise only in those parts or systems of the body that are stressed by the exercise

transfer of learning: the gain or loss in proficiency on one task as a result of practice or experience on another task

tweak: to injure, as in a tweaked finger tendon

variable practice: practice in which many variations of a class of actions are performed; opposite of blocked practice

vein: a blood vessel that conveys blood from the tissue back to the heart (venous return)

visualization: controlled and directed imagery that can be used for awareness building, monitoring and self-regulation, healing, and most importantly, as a kind of mental programming for good performances

wired: completely figured out, as in a wired route

working: practicing the moves on a difficult route, either through top roping or hangdogging

References

Bell, Keith F. (1983). *Championship Thinking*. Englewood Cliffs, NJ: Prentice-Hall, Inc.

Bompa, Tudor O. (1983). *Theory and Methodology of Training*. Dubuque, IA: Kendall/Hunt Publishing Co.

Copper, Robert. (1989). *Health & Fitness Excellence*. Boston, MA: Houghton Mifflin Co.

Covey, Stephen R. (1990). *The 7 Habits of Highly Effective People*. New York, NY: Simon & Schuster.

Guthrie, Helen A. (1983). *Introductory Nutrition*. St. Louis, MO: Mosby Co.

Harris, Dorothy V., & Harris, Bette L. (1984). *Sports Psychology: Mental Skills for Physical People*. New York, NY: Leisure Press.

Hass, Robert. (1983). *Eat To Win*. New York, NY: Signet.

Kubistant, Tom. (1986). *Performing Your Best*. Champaign, IL: Leisure Press.

Loehr, James E. (1986). *Mental Toughness Training for Sports*. Lexington, KY: Stephen Green Press.

Long, John (1991). *Face Climbing*. Evergreen, CO: Chockstone Press.

Meager, Jack. (1990). *Sports Massage*. Barrytown, NY: Station Hill Press.

Nideffer, Robert M. (1985) *Athlete's Guide to Mental Training*. Champaign, IL: Human Kinetics.

Schmidt, Richard B. (1991). *Motor Learning and Performance, From Principles to Practice*. Champaign, IL: Human Kinetics.

Schmidt, Richard B. (1988). *Motor Control and Learning, A Behavioral Emphasis*. Champaign, IL: Human Kinetics.

Southmayd, William & Hoffman, Marshall (1981). *Sports Health: The Complete Book of Athletic Injuries*. New York, NY: Perigee Books.

Tortora, Gerard J. (1983). *Principles of Human Anatomy*. New York, NY: Harper & Row Publishers.

Williams, Melvin H. (1989). *Beyond Training*. Champaign, IL: Leisure Press.